AMERICA FINALLY TELLS THE TRUMP

Coleman G. Lauderdale

2020

Racism Anonymous: America Finally Tells the Trump

Racism Anonymous: America Finally Tells the Trump / Lauderdale, Coleman G. / Non-Fiction

ISBN: 978-0-578-46069-7

For permission requests, please visit
www.TheSupreminati.com.

Table of Content

Acknowledgment

I especially want to thank all those who inspired me to write this book. My influences are from A wide range of people. The Most Current being: Dr. Claude Anderson, Ken O'Keefe, The Activist. David Icke, Dr. Boyce Watkins, Robert David Steel and of course the Minister. The One who's name alone might frighten some Jewish and whites from reading this book. All the life experiences, past and present conditions, that I draw knowledge from are extremely valuable to me. They make up the canvass that provides the perspective that I operate from and aim to share with you in these writings.

I also want to thank the African American editor who would not edit my book. Consequently, she motivated me in different ways, although not intentionally. She told me I wasn't credible enough, and I quote:

"As the author of a non-fiction book, you effectively describe the problem. In order for the reader to trust your proposed solutions to the problem, he or she depends on the authority of the author and/or the factual sources on which the solutions are based. Are you an educator, a social science professional, or do you possess credentials that lend credibility to your opinions? In other words, give the reader a reason to buy your book and adopt your solutions. Everyone has the right to express opinions, but when those opinions are for sale (in book form), the buyer is extremely critical in deciding what to expect. I would not be the best editor for your book because I do not feel the material has a strong narrative voice."

My initial thought was something that rhymed with Chuck Foo, but I decided that I would *respond* to her instead of *reacting* to her. I realized that she was right. People are more inclined to lend credence to professionals; those who are well-studied and recognized by a prevalent college or Ivy-league university in the form of a bachelor's, master's, or a doctorate in their field of concentration. Therefore, allow me to say this: I am merely expressing my viewpoint. I am not hoping to sell or persuade you, the reader. I am exercising my right to free speech. Maybe you will find interest in how I look at things.

I spent a lot of time thinking about writing this book. After a considerable amount of pondering on it, I concluded that my previous editor was right in line with tradition. That, yes, if I was aiming to align and conform with tradition, then I should consider adjusting based on her assessments, but I wasn't in concert with tradition. I didn't intend to be. In fact, my life had been ripped away from the cloth of tradition ever since I was a child, which caused me to view things I learned suspiciously.

To be honest, I now believe much of what America has taught me is a lie. The history I learned is slanted. It seems most of the things we talked about have another version, another side, that appears closer to the truth than the way the schools taught me about them.

I trust that formal education is good, and I applaud those who have put in work to receive theirs, but the reality is they have read a lot of books to learn what they know. I, on the other hand, draw vastly from the life I've lived as my education. No, I didn't receive degrees from the School of Hard Knocks that I am drawing from. Neither were bachelor's, master's, or doctorate degrees awarded. Only blood, sweat, and tears serve as the recognition for the time put in and the hard-fought lessons learned.

I will admit that the educated scholar who, if they attempt to describe this type of story, would more likely display a better use and flow of the English language than I; they would more likely understand book formatting and proper writing etiquette better than I do. Still, that doesn't give their presentation more credence, authenticity, validity, or reality than mine.

I am not going to obtain any more schooling to publish this book. For what it's worth, I stumbled upon two associate degrees while taking college classes in prison. They are both in general studies from Blackhawk College in East Moline, Illinois. Blackhawk offered courses to Logan and Lincoln correctional centers; I served time at both.

I will, at least, try and meet the traditional ideology of proper writing halfway. I will preference many statements with qualifiers like:

- "I believe,"
- "It seems," and
- "It appears."

These will acknowledge my use to pronounce further that these writings are simply my viewpoint:

what I see and believe mostly—kind of like a movie. It is the director's point of view. Hopefully, the substance introduced from my viewpoint will present you with a great piece of writing.

One of the core messages of this book is why, and how, I believe tradition has been part of the culprit to the oppressed state of black lives in America.

Furthermore, I believe tradition has disappointed our youth considerably; they seem to have truly little or no trust in authorities.

There is a New America out there that I envision. "New Americans" care more about grassroots movements than they do the status quo. I'm 56 years of age, and I hope my baby-boomer generation and the generation of yesterday tune in to what I believe is a reality. It would really help this terrible disconnect I believe we currently have with many of our youth.

Today's youth are not totally the same as us regarding their belief system. While the youth of today are the product of our generation, they are now more radical, less patient, no-nonsense, mentally-faster (thanks to tech and video games), independent and (thanks to the Internet) vastly more tech-savvy. All of this makes them somewhat more global-minded, as opposed to boomers who were content to read and clip coupons from their local paper, listen to local radio stations, and watch the local news for information about the happenings in the society.

Introduction

I've lived my entire life in this land called America. This place is the only place I've ever known, labeled as "land of the free and home of the brave." I've heard that compared to many other countries that live under communism, socialism, or other forms of dictatorship, America's constitution offers us freedom many countries don't have. Which is why so many people wanted to come here, I thought.

Through all the roses that seem to represent the beauty this country has to offer, deep inside, it has some rot that is as old as its birth. This rot has stunk up the country for centuries. The smell has now shown itself. We have reached the time where the roses have been overtaken by the rotten weeds that have stunk up this country for centuries. That is

America's garden. Everything in it, America planted, yet I am amazed sometimes at how this country reacts towards its very own sow. Although America offers opportunities and human rights that others from abroad may think of as privileges, still, I think it is perhaps the greatest country to live in by comparison.

In my honest opinion, greed is the true culprit that destroys the morale in this country. How can life be fair if so few of the people have a large majority of the money and resources? I hope I can reach many white Americans in general. (I'm talking about the *non-racist white folks*.) I also hope it will not be too difficult for many of them to complete this book.

In my own life, I found that when having conversations referencing sensitive racial topics with some of my white friends in the past, they seemed to have a difficult time simply receiving information from me. (I'm talking about *truths* I spoke of, not opinions.) If I spoke about cruelties committed against blacks during slavery and the Jim Crow era, I observed they would try and lessen the impact by comparing it to another situation, like The Jewish Holocaust and Hitler. Perhaps, they'd say something like, "Other races were enslaved throughout history as well."

If I pointed out examples of how I believe the systemic racism and social engineering is primarily responsible for the behavior we see or witness in Black communities across the U.S., they would counter with information that points to how some of the blacks are inflicting these conditions upon themselves. Like black-on-black crime. To me, it seemed like they felt they were obligated to rebut as if what I was stating was an objection to something—an insult to *their* America.

Have you ever noticed hardly anyone ever admits to being a racist? I'm not talking about the KKK and the self-proclaimed racist groups out there. I'm talking about regular folks—people who work in typical jobs that require consistent interaction with the general public. No one seems to own up to being part of the systemic and institutional racism that is dominating our society. It's so ironic to me. All the racism I deal with every day, but nobody is a racist.

The more I encounter this situation with white people, the questions that form in my mind are: Do some whites think we are just whining about spilled milk? Do they think blacks just want to complain and "rise up" at any and every opportunity to cry about racism? Or, do they really think blacks, with all their experiences dealing with racism, are not intelligent enough to clearly understand the source of our generational and daily pain, or that most of all—after dealing with racism for more than 700 years—blacks are *still* not clear on what racism looks and feels like?

Some whites would come across as if they understood those events better; that I was not looking at it the right way. Considering blacks are the ones bearing the pain from these occurrences, I find it weird some whites could think they understand racism better. Moreover, it's led me to try and speak on this subject to influence a mending process that will be beneficial for us all. Because I honestly believe there is a Supreminati group with an agenda to depopulate the world, put us under mind control, and clone us *as hi-tech indentured servants*. Most of us, no matter what race or economic class we belong to, are still not members of their *exclusive international club*.

I am talking about the group that *really* influences our daily lives. They control what we see, hear, eat, and consume. The control is not from the president or the free market. This group is so high and powerful, even the president is not allowed in their meetings. For example, think of Jesus at the table with His 12 apostles. Well, The Supreminati is like Satan at the table with his group. They are rooted in the banking sector. I believe the head of the snake has access to unlimited money, like the federal reserve and the Rothschilds. The head of this snake is of Masonic, Zionist, Jesuit, and white supremacist influence. I call them "The Supreminati."

There has been much damage done to blacks in America, and this book will touch on many of those instances. They are all *documented truths*. In my understanding of history, they are events that happened. As a result of some of these things, at times, I may seem angry. At times I may also sound hurt. The truth is, I am wounded, and sometimes, I get furious about the whole situation.

As a man born and raised here in America, can I please share my honest feelings with the whites in general who are reading this book? Can you listen (or read) without countering or rebutting in your mind until you finish? Can you read the words of a scarred Black person who might sound a little irate at times?

Like a doctor (non-racist white people), can you just receive the information about the injuries and hurt I feel in my body before you make a diagnosis? They are the psychological injuries that came from the damages of White Supremacy: historical slavery and Jim Crow.

After reading (hearing me out), you can:

1) Diagnose the situation, and
2) Give your prognosis.

However, first, like a caring doctor would do, read on, and allow me to present all the information. Think about it like this: if you are unable to hear my pain in its entirety, without getting emotionally disturbed because the data is hard to digest, then are you capable of having a thorough and honest assessment of the Black experience?

I realize I am a victim of black-on-black crimes; I don't need to be reminded of this. I'd like to explore that topic in-depth another time. For now, though, can I vent what is real to me, as it relates to my experience with White Supremacy in America?

Often in this book, the carnal man in me is speaking. In the flesh, I feel angry sometimes, but considering and believing in my Savior, I am as assured as Dr. King that He that is in me is greater than he (me) that is in the world.

I am a black man, so if it appears I have bought into a multi-race paradigm based on skin color, then *please* excuse me; I have not. That is not my aim because I would then be perpetuating the same evil myth that the white supremacists use to divide us.

As the one being oppressed, I am naturally defensive at times. Since the oppressor has rendered me the oppressed (victim), it is rational that the carnal man in me resort to a divisive mindset. *Remember, I am the re-action, not the first action.* If, through my passion, the carnal man sticks out, please accept I have learned that such a belief is the root of the ugliness that fuels the very racism I undoubtedly hate. Even though the oppressors have relegated me into what they view as the sub-human Black group, I refuse to own this separation. To do so only perpetuates the same divisive practices I am totally against.

Blacks endured over 400 years of slavery, cross-burnings, and lynching. I hope whites, in general, will at least try to tolerate and spare an hour or two listening or reading about how a black person feels about those experiences. I don't presume to selfishly ask for your time. I welcome all your feedback on the website: www.thesupreminati.com. Click on the Forum, and please give it your thoughtful input and be part of a greater solution.

I suppose real dialogue provides baby steps to get past this racial stalemate we have endured for decades in this country. Isn't it time we try something new? Real discourse, for instance. I don't mean the light surface stuff; I mean the very deep and painful subjects.

I honestly believe there is some generational guilt that needs healing amongst some of the white people. Have you ever seen on CNN, FOX, or MSNBC, where they have a panel of liberals and conservative hosts a guest discussing a racial event that happened in this country? Or maybe even something Donald Trump once said that sounded racist? I notice there is always a *race rationalist* on the panel. To this person, racism just cannot be the motivating factor. This rationalist seems to have many different justifications for why an incident (really) happened. Oddly, racism is not one of them. They just cannot bring themselves to even consider racism is what influenced the event.

Race rationalists are also part of the problem for me. They strike me as people who have a knack for creating alibies for those who commit hate crimes.

I meet white people regularly, and over time, I have

had many interactions and working relationships with these friends, business partners, and co-workers. I can honestly say I believe some of them absolutely hate what their ancestors did to black people. Likewise, some are totally embarrassed and remorseful. They truly seem to hate having to live under the evil cloud of atrocious their ancestors left. This guilt-by-association appears to have made some of them victims in their own persona. These non-racist whites are unfairly connected (by skin color only) to the evil history of slavery and Jim Crowism committed by supremacists that exploited their race via *white exceptionalism*. I feel for them.

There are many racially charged events that we see today. They serve as salt in the wound for black people. The outrage of blacks probably gives the impression that blacks will never let it go, that black people will forever wear history on their sleeves and have a chip on their shoulders. This attitude makes it much harder for all of us to get past racism.

I want white Americans to understand that I would rather that a racial event not inflict me. I don't want to march or to protest; I want to simply have a life (or existence) that is fair. In truth, I would instead love my neighbor than to protest for *social justice.*

I will say that I have a special place in my heart for whites who do not have the hate and racist characteristic of many who came before them. You didn't accept what earlier generations passed down; to me, that's huge. It would be easier for you to go with the flow; however, you rejected the hate getting taught both in words and deeds.

To me, you don't deserve to be unfairly connected to that evil history simply because of your skin color; you had absolutely nothing to do with it. Neither does your heart and soul resemble those of many from your hue—past, and present. I also believe there should be a way to recognize these people in our society. I think resisting the evil hatred taught through generations by their ancestors is worth some type of recognition for people of all skin types. I salute you all!

John Brown, <u>a white abolitionist</u>, fought and killed many whites in the name of justice for black people. Perhaps the most famous white person involved in the abolitionist movement for fighting against slavery in America, leading to the Civil War, he was hung in 1859. Personally, I feel his statue should be the one standing in Charlottesville instead of Robert E. Lee (whom Trump praises).

I hope making it through this book will help with alleviating the generational guilt I believe exists within many whites. The reason I suppose it will be hard for many white readers to get through this book is because some of the topics are hard to admit. For example, an issue that is hard for me to accept is that blacks from Africa sold other blacks into slavery. I hate hearing this, but it's the truth. I also think it epitomizes man's inhumanity to man. Sometimes the truth punches us ridiculously hard; it becomes hard to breathe, hard to live as though the punch never landed.

I am asking the white Americans who may be reading this book to understand some truths about our history and your ancestors. Some of these truths may startle you. You won't like getting punched in the gut, and you will be inclined to turn the book off. I hope you don't. Besides, we all know that healing comes after the pain, and from your healing comes the blessings. I'm still trying to heal. Try and hear me through my wounds.

Thirty-seven years later, after being convicted and going to prison for the first time, I am feeling the punishment more now than ever. The episode of doing six years of imprisonment wore off a long time ago. In fact, I don't think that incident was even the intended punishment. The real punishment was a life of dis-enfranchisement that I now live. The six years were like the prelude to the sentence.

I am blown away and astonished by how this country treats my past conviction. America treats it like it just happened yesterday. In the job market, a background check is the deal-breaker. To be a sanitation worker or a fireman who goes into burning buildings, I'm disqualified. To save lives and properties, they say no because of a conviction that happened 37 years ago. What harm can a man do by going into a burning building to end fire or to save someone's life? What damage can be done cleaning up garbage off the street? That led me to the conclusion that the penal system isn't about correcting lives as in their name description Department of Corrections. If it was, then they obviously don't believe in their own product. No, this is bigger than that. The officer who arrested me, and the judge who sentenced me, are no longer in the picture, but the punishment, humiliation, and emotional torture continue. Who is applying the pressure now?

I am convinced that our criminal justice system's agenda is not only about un-fair sentencing and overwhelmingly incarcerating black men, which represents a moment or an event in that person's life. The Criminal Justice system seems to have a long-term vision for the punishment they give.

The Justice system, as evidenced, is cunningly engineering permanent long-term damage on black men and removing them from productive class citizenship to permanent under-class citizenship that adds no value or growth to the society. To do what with, I ask, and who is it that is really orchestrating this?

What's interesting is that before 2008, the background check wasn't as enforced as it is now. Suddenly, the Patriot Act changed the entire complexion of this country. It took away our right to privacy; we became a police state. Gradually, the country seems to be taking up some elements of communism. Then I started to put it all together, and

I realized that as painful and as damaging as my incarceration process was to me, it was essentially a minute piece to a much grander scheme. That scheme is to add me to the permanent underclass of black men. I ask again, to do what with?

While my life means everything to me, it's nothing to those who seem to be orchestrating this grand scheme. While I was thinking that doing time was paying my debt to society, little did I know that doing time was only a down payment. Paying my debt to society didn't begin until I was released.

When I look up the word Republic in the dictionary, it reads: "A state in which the supreme power rests in the body of citizens entitled to vote and is exercised by representatives chosen directly or indirectly by them." When I look up the word democracy in the dictionary, it reads: "Government by the people; a form of government in which the supreme power is vested on the people and exercised directly by them or by their elected agents under a free electoral system." That sounds like the same meaning to me, so I curiously asked this question: why is there a two-party system of Democrats and Republicans? I became very suspicious of our government.

First and foremost, I thought of our government as guardians of the Constitution, who would regulate the electoral process and uphold the amendments. In doing so, I believed this would undergird our existence with a virtue that would not allow corruption to permeate our lives. Unfortunately, I was wrong. My views about this government have since changed.

I'll start with the U.S. Supreme Court justices. To vote Citizens United into law was the straw that broke my back with regards to trying to believe in our political system. That really caused me to think that the political process is like a dog and pony show. Along with other frivolous moves, like installing Justice Clarence Thomas, and most recently the confirmation of Justice Bret Kavanaugh, why was there such a rush with no patience to gather information and evaluate his background? I'm convinced that Oligarchy rules this country—perhaps the super-wealthy families, or what I call The Supreminati.

The nine justices that we call the Supreme Court should have the verbiage changed regarding their job description. I honestly don't really know the exact verbiage that details their job duties, but if El Choppo, Kim Jung Un, or Vladimir Putin can finance a political campaign—whereas the campaign can lawfully keep in secret the identity of these contributors—and our supreme court justices approve, and by default, mandates this type of politics, then should I view this group of judges as an authority on Justice? Supreme Justice? Well, I don't. Pardon me, but this (to me) is turning a blind eye to corruption. Therefore, I cannot trust the institution of the Supreme Court.

I now describe the political system as a scam. Mainly because the system deliberately projects to the people an electoral process that appears fair, but they know it is not. That deception is what scam artists do exactly: "They have *good game*," as we would say.

The two-party system I mentioned earlier, to me, is just an appearance, a decoy, or a mere cover-up for the agenda of the real rulers of this country, or this empire. There is only a one-party system with Supreme Rulership in this country, I believe. That one party is what I will call "The Supreminati." They have strategically conditioned the public to first believe in the two-party system, then behave accordingly as a Democrat or a Republican. While we go on living our lives under this deceptive two-party system, the American eagle, the Oligarchy, or what I call "The Supreminati," is the one party that really rules the most important affairs of this nation.

To me, this Oligarchy and/or The Supreminati is the

eagle. The eagle's agenda is paramount in this country. That is the Party with empirical power. Not the Democrats for four to eight years, then a switch to the Republicans for another four to eight years. That's just the eagle rotating its wings.

The eagle has two wings, the right wing for Republicans, and left for Democrats. These wings seem to alternate occupying the people's attention, preventing most of them from looking at what the eagle is up to. *Or should I say The Supreminati?*

Imagine a bird's wings are fighting each other. I think it's a trick. We, as people, should pay more attention to "the Eagle," The Supreminati, and the Oligarch. The eagle is more than brilliant. It can be challenging to pay attention to them because the media does not talk about them like this. They own the media; at the tip of that Pyramid is where the rulers are. (Basically, the same group of people controls FOX and CNN.) Democrats and Republicans are beneath the point of that Pyramid.

When trying to pay attention, people really do think the wings are fighting each other. Maybe they are, or perhaps the eagle instigated the fight to entertain us, or the Oligarchs may just be playing us. There is nothing Americans love most than seeing a good fight. That's why boxing phenom Floyd Mayweather is so rich. We pay good amounts of money just to watch a match. That is why CNN and FOX are completely different stations. In essence, and by design, only a one-party system. That party is The Supreminati, and we are paying with our lives.

You often hear people say things like "the Democrats did this," or "the Republicans did that," as if those are the only two powers. They say the greatest trick the devil ever pulled was convincing the world that he didn't exist. This reference to the powers is a perfect example of that. We never talk about the eagle itself. Only what its right wing or it's left wing is doing.

If America is the first country to experiment with the use of democracy in a voting system, then kudos to America for its effort to give people a say in rulership and government; the birth of the Constitution, in 1789, was a remarkable achievement. Ideally, I believe it was, and is, the only way to pursue fairness and equality for everyone.

Can you imagine following the direct rule of a King and Queen or a dictator here in America? However, when constructing the Constitution, there seems to have been an absence of a spiritual and divine influence emanating from a Benevolent Power. Given the bloodshed of Native Americans and slavery, when the Constitution rolled off the printing press, I believe it was stained.

There is an element of danger that comes with talking about The Supreminati and bringing people together. I can think of some throughout history who have had strange circumstances surrounding their deaths. It seems that when they began speaking out against The Supreminati, something happened to them. You show me a man in history, black or white, who's movement was aimed at bringing people together, and I will (more than likely) show a man who was assassinated or died "mysteriously."

When I hear anyone speaking of The Supreminati, its usually in the context of a secret group of wealthy and powerful people who rule the world and work diligently to inconspicuously keep people divided and in the dark about the real realities in our lives. To me, they are described the same way the devil is. They are said to operate in the shadows. They are said to be the real power behind the scenes, seeking rulership and autonomy over our lives. Using money and shiny things to lure and manipulate every aspect of our existence, they are described as satanic and cunning.

I'm not writing this book to simply point the finger at the wrong things the white supremacists, nationalists, and racists have done to black people in this country. That is not my intention. My hope is to see *the love that could be* moved into humanity and bring people closer to each other. I believe a race/class war is on deck here in America, maybe around the world, and I genuinely believe the world is sick of this stranglehold that The Supreminati seem to have on these nations and the world at large.

I've read a little about these secret groups of wealthy and powerful elites who are said to rule our daily existence like puppet masters that we never really see. The way I see it, the body that each of them lives in, is a self-healing machine connected to a higher power; actually, a lower power, yet a power, nonetheless. I've never read or heard any claims that Lucifer, Satan, or Baphomet created them. From everything I've read or heard, they claim to believe that these forces enlighten or illuminate them, not to have created them.

The Higher Power I have faith in created the

heavens and the earth to be self-healing cells or atmospheres. If *population control* is the objective of these dark forces, and their goal is to eliminate billions of people from the earth, then I would say that they have claimed ownership of this world. They seem to have decided that ruling the earth is their function, if not their birthright. They are playing God; that's deep.

These dark forces have been accused of staging false flag wars to justify attacks and killings all over the world. Analysts indicate that World War III will be nuclear. I wonder what they think might happen afterward. Atomic war will kill plants, wildlife, and aquatic sea life in addition to human life. Nuclear war will contaminate the air that we all breathe. Assuming the earth is said to have been here more than 4.5 billion years (Wikipedia), I guess it knows how to repair itself of any foul elements that try to damage it. *Just sayin'.*

I bet the earth is more of a self-healing machine than

the human body is. The control over the world these people seem to be after is probably way above their heads. I tell you; their devil is lying to them. Do they think God will not find them in their secret underground bunkers?

When I think of FEMA camps, underground bunkers, MK-ultra mind control, real ID's, fake news, child sex slaves and trafficking, nuclear wars, martial law, and all the compelling indicators that seem to speak to the notion that something very powerful and covert is being prepared for, I pray for a Higher Power to intervene immediately and forcefully. Sadly, the ongoing methods used through media to act as decoys to keep the masses occupied in an artificial reality (born of an artificial narrative) are working masterfully. The most realistic thread that runs through this false reality is that we are not paying attention to what they (The Eagle) are doing—I mean The Supreminati. The shiny objects occupy us; we are too busy swatting flies, and the crocodiles are biting.

I can only believe that many in these secret groups have come to know that what they are doing is horrible. I've listened to a few ex-Illuminati members talk about the atrocious and inhumane experiences that led them to defect from the secret group. I guess most are probably in too deep, and I hear they sign their contracts with blood, and death is the only way out for them.

To me, when someone loses the fear of dying, they may be able to tap into another power, with or without their breath. I've sometimes wondered if an individual wanted out, confessed to God the remorse they felt for being involved with Satan's demonic practices, then went ahead to kill themselves (suicide), would God bless their soul.

Nevertheless

Whether it's pre-destiny or freewill, blacks being closer to God is where the result of man's time on Earth seems to have led us. If this is the result of the episode of life we live, then I believe this is the chosen will of God, our Creator. Over time, I have brought myself to thank Him for all the pain, tears, and bloodshed it took to bring black people closer to Him. Yes, we've suffered immensely, but so did Jesus Christ—God's only begotten Son.

If many blacks had never experienced the horrific acts of slavery, Jim Crow laws, and oppression committed here in the U.S., would they have risen to greatness in this country to the levels we have? *I'm not so sure.*

Blacks have endured and accomplished many great things. Look at the many wealthy, rich, powerful, and influential black people around the universe. Through it all, black greatness blossomed, and just maybe soared higher because of those tragedies. I'm certainly not making light of the atrocities suffered by my people here in this country, but sometimes the height of greatness is fueled by the depth of the pain. Many blacks now have money, resources, and power to begin an effort to counter the horrible acts that were perpetuated (predominantly) by The Supreminati in this country.

When I look at blacks from many other countries, the U.S. seems to have the highest percentage who have both accomplished goals and amassed significant wealth. We have a substantial number of rich black people in this country, whether my people are accomplished or not. We might have more advanced blacks (percentage-wise) in a capitalist society than blacks from abroad. Whether it be sports, entertainment, or whatever, blacks have the spending power north of one trillion dollars. (Statistical)

We have many who are in the church seeking God. Collectively, Black America has tremendous resources, and many of us probably share an emotional connection to the plight of black people here in the U.S. Blacks can actually pool their money, resources, talents, and influences together and shock the current state of black life off its present axis to epically change the outcome for the next generation of black families; however, more importantly, we need to change the state of black life *now*.

The surest and safest way of improving the conditions of our youth is to obtain a higher education, which is the most practical way of achieving a successful future. Whether the degree leads to a job in the workforce, or entrepreneurship in the marketplace, this is the only thing that can be attained. The later, no one can come back to take it away.

Getting an education is yours to keep forever. The average black youth may not excel in sports, acting, singing, or music, so the safest way is to obtain higher education and acquire a career or significant skill. That is, of course, to have a brighter future and a better tomorrow. However, this does not address the huge void of present-day fatherless black families, economic oppression, black-on-black killings, and the dismal conditions we see today in black communities across the United States. Neither does it address the present issue of mending the relationship between black men and black women, which in my opinion, is the area of damage that most importantly needs repairing to fix the current conditions of the black family and the community. Black men and black women loving each other is the core problem. It is the root failure of all the conditions we see in black people, their community, and the entire black race.

Likewise, I'm a little perplexed when I think about some of our rich and famous black people today. I've read and listened to many videos about how "The Supreminati" controls the entertainment industry. There is much talk about how some popular celebrities sell their souls to the devil to obtain and maintain fortune or fame. Some believe that once these entertainers cross a financial threshold, they must take an oath. It is even said that pledges and sacrifices are required.

I hear about rituals that must be practiced, and some of the stories I've heard about these alleged rituals are really sickening, totally wicked, and demonic. I see plenty of symbolism put on by entertainers in the music, movies, and sports industries. I have seen hand gestures, even Baphomet-looking outfits. I've also heard celebrities (black and white) talk about the evil spirits that seem to rule behind the scenes.

Have you seen the hand signs on some of the photos taken by many blacks in the media? Hand signs that are associated with the Illuminati? I see it a lot—famous black people that I appreciate and have great respect for, displaying mysterious hand signals and photos with one eye covered, which is said to be a sign of the Illuminati. These things trouble me.

I admit I am disturbed because some of our most popular blacks are alleged to be part of these secret groups. I won't shout out any of their names but think of some of the prevalent blacks in music, movies, media, and even sports. Many of them are thought to be puppets of the Illuminati. I can honestly say that I have seen many photos of them with those hand signs. This, to me, means that seeing these signs regularly cannot be just a coincidence.

I've heard that one of the conditions or rules laid out for black people in these groups is that they are prohibited from financing any major programs that will uplift black communities in the United States. Have you noticed that few of them seem to donate or have programs in foreign countries? Look around at the black millionaires in sports, music, and movies. Consider the fact that there seem to be few programs in black communities from these black multi-millionaires. It does raise the likelihood of whether this prohibition is valid. If it is true that they must sign such an oath that forbids programs that would help uplift the black communities in the U.S., then that's incredibly sad and disheartening.

These people fear to lose their money, reputation, and resources from those who are believed to control the industries. Remember the movie "Enemy of the State" starring Will Smith? Think of the scenes when they were destroying his life: freezing his bank accounts, destroying his home, and putting articles in the newspaper about him. The Supreminati is said to have this kind of power. They can ruin any celebrity's life, allegedly at will.

These circumstances could really put many black celebrities in a precarious situation. Think about it. If you were in their position, would you speak out against the Illuminati? I often hear they sign contracts with blood. They are said to have power in media, banking, politics, law enforcement, and courtrooms; they are known to be cunning. Would you want this evil satanic force after you? I don't think anyone could challenge this group individually. Maybe, one day, people will God-up together and take it to them. That probably would be the only way people can overcome them.

There is an immediate need to begin repairing and reconciling the black man and the black woman's relationship. Black men need to be respected again. You see, without addressing this, young black children will lack the rearing necessary to prepare for that "better tomorrow." While there are exceptional cases of people overcoming incredible odds to turn out to be a great success story, most people will need a support base when starting out. If the household they live in lacks an adequate support base, then it is highly unlikely that they will function at a level that allows them to overachieve, or even achieve anything at all.

For many years, blacks have talked about attaining a better future for themselves; however, herein lies the problem:

The matter needs *emergency-like* attention. There must be a drastic, immediate, and deliberate act to shock the present State of Black Life from its current axis to another dimension. Isolated gradual independent efforts will only have a little impact— *something must shock the State of Black Life.* The ripple effect of decades of damage is too big. The interrupter, or antagonist must be mammoth.

What Do You Think?

I am so frustrated with racism and hate. I've come to believe that blacks have exhausted every possible way to combat, compromise, and plead for racism to end in the country. I no longer think it's possible without the help of committed white Americans; specifically, the truly non-racist white people.

There is cancer in the white race, and ordinary white people, in general, know those who are cut from that cloth. They should condemn them publicly and privately. If regular, committed white Americans joined in eradicating the ones who are racists, the cancer of racism would be on an express lane out of our lives, and the society will only see racism in the rear-view mirror.

I had this idea for an organization called Racism Anonymous. Racism is an illness, isn't it? Such as the many "-isms" we live with every day that needs treatment. We are yet to view and approach it like the illness that it is. In fact, many whites won't even admit they have a disease. Think about it; other than the Klan (white Nazis) and known supremacist groups that wear it proudly on their sleeves, not many whites seem to own up to being racists. So, it appears that the self-proclaimed groups are where all the racism comes from in our society.

I imagine there are many whites in the closet, and sadly enough, there are way too many who may not even recognize the racist element I believe lives within them. Racism Anonymous would be world-changing only if the non-racist white people subscribe to it. Non-racist whites could work to eradicate those who represent evil amongst them. They should also be willing to take an honest look at themselves. Let blacks help you to understand how racism birthed white privilege and how it serves as a reminder that keeps the pain of racism at the forefront of black consciousness.

With a program like this, I imagine love would find its way back into humanity. (As in, love thy neighbor.) Initial benefactors would be ordinary white people in general and the non-racist whites. If they hated Euro-centric racism the way black people hate Euro-centric racism and decided to condemn those who demonstrated such characteristics, attitudes, and behaviors, things would change fast.

I would like to see an organization set up to deliberately destroy racism—an organization like Alcoholics Anonymous or Narcotics Anonymous. Is racism an illness? If it is, then let's treat it as such.

I would also like to know how whites, in general, would react to a program like this. Explicitly, all nationalities for that matter. Give us your opinion on a program like this at www.thesupreminati.com. Click on the Forum and tell us what you think or your contributions.

Arterpretation

Our interpretation of our environment is actually the design or "artwork" of The Supreminati. Their experimentation manufacturing and engineering of the outcome and behavior they want to see is what I call "arterpretation." The material I present is, unfortunately, not comical, happy, or pleasant. To me, it is the raw realities that undergird the mirage of the beautiful American dream—that they keep selling to the masses. Therefore, it is not for the faint of heart. If you are someone with few trials and adversities in your life, you may find it hard to make it through this book. While many topics evoke anger, depression, and maybe sadness, they are necessary to pave a way to the hope and light that complete the story.

I hope my viewpoint will be enlightening for many.

Other than my own experiences, most of the subjects here are common knowledge, but it is also my viewpoint that I strive to introduce to you. My aim is not to come off as just another black tale about the injustices suffered by black people throughout the history of this country. Nor do I want to encourage blacks to be angry with white supremacists, though I will demonstrate the role white supremacists played in setting the stage and socially engineering black people to be in the conditions they are presently in.

The spoils of racism are central to the evolution of the black man and woman's failure in their journey to become a healthy and productive family union. Therefore, to exclude or lessen its consistency throughout the history of black people, would, in my opinion, be like diluting the complete story. For the most part, we are going to look simply at some past events and relate them to the conditions and behavior we see today.

I have lived my life this far in a world that has altered my reality. I could understand cinematography and how Hollywood studios create a setting with a backdrop that would project to the viewer the image that best pronounces the intent that the story is trying to convey, but I never considered it until recently how this technique of cinematography applies to my life.

The atmosphere that I was subjugated to while growing up was placed around me by design. I used to think that the decision-making of my parents and their parents were the primary reasons I landed in an environment that shaped my views, my perception, and my outlook on the world. Now, I think my parent's decision-making was secondary at best. I believe they were unknowingly faced with an altered reality to begin with. I now see, at the core, how cinematography got applied to black life in the U.S.—perhaps all lives, but blacks especially.

Maybe Shakespeare was right when he said, "All

the world is a stage, and all the men and women are merely actors." I honestly believe the Oligarchs and/or The Supreminati, the people that fundamentally control and influence what we see and hear, have created a stage in the world we live in. On that stage, we go about our daily lives without knowing a stage was set for us to live on.

While I presume the stage was set to condition, engineer, project, and manufacture many different beliefs and behaviors, particularly within the black community, the most painful and damaging to the black community and family is that the script was written with a bullseye. There has been an intent to destroy the black man deliberately and relentlessly through cunning imagery, direct and blatant injustices, and any other possible means. The agenda is, and always will be, to never stop destroying the black man and, by extension, the black family and community.

The executive producers, directors, and outlets of

this "Cinemania" collectively synergize and laser in the bullseye to destroy the black man fulltime, which is a means to discredit him, his dignity, his role in the society, his potential, and even his reason for being on earth. *I believe this from the bottom of my heart.*

Before I give examples to support my position on this, let me first caution black women: it is not my intention to lessen nor challenge your contribution, strength, or your extraordinary resilience throughout Black History in this country. I must say, with no lack of gratitude, you held the black community up on its feet. I can't help but love and appreciate black women for this. It is because of their strength, evidence of my mother's strength to press on, that I can sit here and write my story.

My father wasn't in my life. I do acknowledge that he provided the sperm that fertilized the egg, and without him, I wouldn't be here today, but birth is just the beginning of the process of developing a new life. He wasn't there to guide me through life's journey. My late mother took full responsibility from birth; as a black woman, so did other black women.

Please accept it, sisters, that the destruction of your man was another reality to co-exist with the burden of single parenting you've borne on your shoulders for so long. I want us to end this BS rhetoric of sisters being stronger than brothers. This psychologically manufactured condition (bullshit) imposed upon us, is designed to keep us at war with each other and hinder our efforts to unify. It's bullshit. It is social engineering at its evil best. I never hear this man vs. women power comparison among any other group of people—just black people. Why?

Thanks to Cinemania, black women are the chosen ones to reign supreme over black men. That is the pre-determined will and agenda of The Supreminati. You are welcomed into privilege in

America as a VIP guest compared to your black male counterpart. In fact, the white supremacist welcomes you so much more than the black man whom they have deliberately suppressed, depressed, weakened, disenfranchised, drugged, incarcerated, murdered, and decimated so bad that you, the black woman, percentage-wise can stand tall as the strongest, the breadwinner, the richest, and the smartest amongst blacks, yet you are single in large numbers. *Get it?*

The *single* part is the void in your life that White Supremacy also engineered. You see, single black women raising black boys was the desired result, not black men raising black boys. While doing so, if the messages the boys receive throughout his life (be it from television, movie images, or perhaps listening to the narrative coming from his often bitter mother and her girlfriends about the shortcomings of black men in general), then he is being brainwashed. An *alternate reality* is getting created; that reality is this: black men are weaker.

In addition to this alternative reality, black population control was another part of The Supreminati's mission. Division equals non-reproduction. Black women received public aid for their children if there wasn't a black man around the house. Think about this for a moment: this act takes the father out of the child's life. (Break the family, and we will pay for it.)

It was crucial that they were, and are, willing to pay to have that reality in place. They financed broken black families *under the guise of public assistance!* That's looking good and doing evil at the same time. The truth we see today in 2020 is overwhelming: single-parenting mothers and fatherless black households. *Surely this alternate reality was paved by movies, media, and even public aid checks given directly to black women.*

I am amazed when I see whites in the media speak

about the overwhelming fatherless black families. They are clueless about what The Supreminati has done to ensure and maintain this condition. That is the design of The Supreminati. An *alternate reality* they have conditioned the world to believe. To a handful of our sisters, the phrase, "drinking the Kool-Aid" comes way short in describing how you are relishing in this superior stature over your brothers. It's more like you are smoking the meth. My frustration is that America has tricked my people. Black family reunions are far and few in between, and there are many important loved ones from our family trees missing.

Did you know on July 6, 1944, baseball great Jackie Robinson <u>refused to sit at the back of the bus</u>? He was a Lieutenant in the military. There was nearly a shoot-out. They didn't tell us about that, did they? They told us about Rosa Parks who, 11 years later, in December 1955, refused to give up her seat and go to the back of the bus. Why didn't they tell us about the black man? About how he stood strong in the face of injustice? Because they would rather tell us and the rest of the world that our black woman is stronger than our black men.

Sisters, do you think I am out to reduce Rosa Park's courage by stating this? Please don't. That would only give glory to the silly competition they have engineered among black men and black women. I am merely pointing out how the consciousness of America will never project the courage and strength of the black man. That part of history is erased— *swept under the rug.*

Did you also know William Stills, known as the Father of the Underground Railroad, is reported to have helped more than 900 slaves to freedom, and Harriet Tubman is reported to have helped around 300? They considered putting her on the $20 bill without even mentioning or recognizing the efforts of William Stills. The Trump administration delayed it. Why not William Stills? Why won't they tell us how the black man performed in the face of imminent danger? Most of us probably never heard his name before because they would rather tell us that throughout history, the black woman was stronger and more courageous than the black man. Stills' part of history did not get mentioned; another ploy to weaken the black man.

America's commitment to tarnishing and killing black men and their great legacies is a manufactured perception. It's a purposeful lie, deception, that alters history and darkens futures. It's the *alternate reality* they create. If you tell a lie thousands of times, people will begin to believe it's the truth. Perception becomes a reality.

I often think about the committee of white men who work daily to upkeep the public's perception of the black man. I remember seeing those old movies with Shirley Temple as a little white girl bossing around and controlling full-grown black men who were portrayed as dumb, cowardly butlers and servants. It was a *master and pet* kind of relationship. What message were those images conveying to the world about black men? All the way up to a blockbuster film like *Rush Hour*. Remember the pool hall scene where the black men (Don Cheadle and Clifton Powell) were running illegal gambling in the back? Also, think about rappers. Why are they all talking about the same topics? Teks, AK's, poppin' bottles, pimping, thugin', moving kilos, bitches, jewelry, cars, mansions, and ballin'?

I often think some foreigners I meet would seem to have a preconceived idea about me as a black man. It wasn't a good perception for me. I would think they received that perception from movies and television. Today, in 2020, when I look at many roles black men have played in film, it says to me that keeping the black man's image a particular way to the public is a career vocation. That is not by chance; it is by design. Someone is working on this project at this very moment.

Think about how the media tarnished the names of our famous black men. I heard Eddie Griffin, the comedian, say black men will not leave the spotlight without an asterisk by their name. (Not an exact quote.) Nevertheless, the point is clear, I hope.

The most powerful and popular black person today is Oprah (doesn't need a last name) Winfrey, a black woman. She is an extraordinary woman, but this, too, is by design. Think about the black man who was probably at one point more influential, wealthier, and more powerful than her in media, who she may have looked up to as a mentor of some sort: Bill Cosby. Where is he? Did he really deserve prison? He wasn't still a threat to the society in his eighties, was he? House arrest would have satisfied correcting him, wouldn't it? That is if correcting him was the primary purpose. Or was the purpose really to destroy him and his positive influence?

To think a strategy was implemented to create an imbalance between the black man and the black woman is unbelievable to fathom. Yet think about what you see today: black families totally being decimated is primarily the work of black people. Now open your eyes to this trickery and don't be fooled. This decimation of the black family is not merely the work of black people; America engineered it.

Thank You, Lord

I honestly believe all things will move to its extreme opposite. Sometimes, this movement is gradual, and other times, it can be faster. Man has ruled the world according to the history of all the great nations. Without question, man is responsible for some remarkable industrial and technological advancements we have in this world.

I assume, from a humanistic and spiritual point of view, man has lost his way, resulting in a world that is morally deficient and has forsaken goodness in exchange for monetary gains. The carnal ambitions of man have weakened his ability to lead and steward God's world, to me—leaving this world wounded and in need of love. Power is shifting to a source that can produce love, and that source is a woman. It is the woman's turn to influence international policies, I believe. Women will impact political affairs more than ever before. In a natural sense, it must be this way because she is needed. This is my belief only.

The earth was created to be self-sufficient, but man is destroying it—its soil, trees, water, wildlife, and air. It is only natural that the earth will correct itself. Remember, it's been here a lot longer than man. Earth is probably saying to itself, "Who are these rookies trying to destroy or kill me? (As in death.) Let me now move into the hands of the one who will care for and nurture me with purpose." Women will bring in more of what this world needs. *I'm just saying.*

America Finally Tells the Trump

I want to take a moment to thank God for Donald J. Trump. While stomaching the time he occupies the presidency is terrible for many, he represents a *transitional moment* in the evolvement of this country. The ugly and treacherous nature of White Supremacy is up for judgment now. It has been brought to the forefront, thanks to President Trump. That is not his intention; it is the by-product of who he is. I cannot remember a time in history when racism and White Supremacy were a topic in news coverage as frequently as it is today. It feels like finally, we have caught the culprit.

I also believe Donald Trump will go down in history for influencing more teens and young adults to get involved with politics and voting. His presidency is the real *National Emergency;* he stunned the nation and alarmed the youth. I am thankful for this. Consider this the good that comes from his presidency. For me, that good is putting white supremacists in a fishbowl. We can all see how ugly and dangerous they are for the world—no more hiding. If Hillary Clinton had won the presidency, it would be business as usual for white supremacists. Their hate and evil would not be as isolated and up for judgment as it is now.

In my view, we've come to a point where racism is no longer something many whites are ashamed of. Before, being a racist was a terrible thing for whites. Now, it's different. It's become somewhat acceptable, or not-so-really-awful to be recognized as one. I credit that to Trump. Look at his audience at his rallies. Aren't they flagrant? How many blatant comments and actions has he shown to suggest he is racist? The most troublesome to me is the supporters. There is no shame; they are riding with him no matter what, and they don't feel guilty about it. It's almost as if many of them can finally publicly say they are proud to be white and racists; America finally tells the Trump.

I feel we are now seeing into the house of America's core; the offspring of the white supremacist ideology comprised the government, the white power structure, and the foundation of this country are of that built America. The onion is peeled. Inside is the root of racism and hate for those who aren't members, especially black people. Again, America finally tells the Trump.

The root of racism seems to be Trump's base. While it got masked for centuries as something to deny or be ashamed of, it is now out of the closet, and some whites are with it, unapologetically proud. They seem to (literally) have a license to be racist. Look around at the gruesome killings of blacks by white police officers; this is nothing new. The only new thing is that technology brought it out of the closet. What was done in the shadows in the past is now seen in the light of cell phones. Now, whites must explain and own up to these occurrences.

For centuries, these incidents went on without people witnessing them. Without cell phones and the Internet, we wouldn't even know about the last 20 killings of black men by white officers. To me, now that the revolution is social medialized, the response from America's law enforcement speaks volumes. Starting with the beating of Rodney King, all the way up to the killing of Laquan McDonald in Chicago (who was shot 16 times by a white cop), to George Floyd (who was literally choked on nationwide TV), it says the same thing—there has been and always will be a green light to destroy black men in every way possible.

To me, whites can get away with anything they perpetuate towards black people; they can beat them, shoot them, and jail them without facing the law or getting punished for it. Basically, this is the freedom they have as white people; this is an element of white privilege. They can even call the president a liar, a nigger, a terrorist, or anything they want if he is black. That is all because White Supremacy backs them. So, to the blacks who fight for Civil Rights, they will compromise occasionally, but when it's all said and done, I doubt if blacks will ever be treated with absolute fairness by white supremacists. Until most whites set out to heal themselves from this disease and join blacks to rid our lives of this cancer of racism (which is pure hate), things will never be fair for all completely.

I agree many whites are slowly joining the cause. The reality has settled in, and even whites, in general, realize they are not down with the degree of hate that comes from White Supremacy. This group seems to be absolute in the fact that you are either with them or not. If you are not, then the hell with you too is how they feel.

For a long time, adults have always complained that more young adults needed to get involved in politics. Well, the youth are more involved than ever before. President Obama brought many young adults into politics with smiles and excitement on their faces. Trump brought more of them out, but they came into the political arena with fear, concern, frustration, and anger.

Overcoming any problem starts with a conversation about the causes. The first step in Alcoholics Anonymous (A.A.) is to first admit one's alcoholism. The media is talking about White Supremacy regularly these days. This represents the beginning to the end of the stranglehold The Supreminati has had on America, perhaps the world.

I thank God for Donald Trump. Where there is a beginning, there is an end. Even ordinary white Americans are getting a better look than ever before. I really don't think non-supremacist whites clearly understood the impact the hate from supremacists had on our existence. They do now.

I believe by the year 2022 (in biblical proportion), something drastic will happen in the world with White Supremacy. This occurrence will impact the entire world—perhaps, Armageddon. I have faith that it will be for the good of all humanity: a redemption of some sort, especially for blacks.

I am also torn with Donald Trump being President. I do believe he is a racist. This, of course, I hate. However, as I continue to learn more about The Deep State and the way they seem to control and influence foreign affairs and international politics, I suspect Trump is unintentionally challenging the stranglehold this powerful secret group of people has on the U.S.. I am glad this is happening. His renegade approach is pulling the curtain back on their powers. From what I understand, The Deep State comes from those three-lettered government agencies: CIA, FBI, and FDA. They are said to have no oversight and seem to stir up much corruption.

Personally, I regard Trump as an accidental President because the presidential elections are simply a dog-and-pony show to give people the *illusion of inclusion*. All presidents are *selected* even before the general elections, or at least narrowed down to a few choices, is my opinion.

Have you ever heard the theory of the bloodline: that all presidents are connected by lineage? I wonder if this is true. We cannot have a real democracy until the candidates who generate the most votes win the election. That cannot happen if there is an Electoral College. I believe the Electoral College creates the latitude for the manipulation of the elections; therefore, it is kind of the trump card that allows for an election to be swayed.

To me, somehow, Hilary Clinton's loss was a screw-up or a mistake. I don't think The Supreminati (the most powerful Oligarchs above The Deep State) planned it this way (for once in our lifetime). Against all their efforts to control the elections,

Donald Trump became the 45th President. Have you noticed how he doesn't fit in? I think this is a good thing. He is not politics as usual. I think we truly needed an odd-ball to shake up American politics. I am not saying he is the exact odd-ball that was required, but American politics needed an overhaul.

While I would never support a racist whom I feel cares nothing for blacks or the lower class, part of me wants to believe his actions are disrupting The Deep State. These government agencies (i.e. FBI, CIA, Secret Service, FDA, etc.) are extremely powerful. Some of them have no oversight and have been accused of doing some terrible things.

President Trump is nothing close to a traditional politician (who follows the status quo). He wants to be like Putin and Kim Jon Yeung; it seems—a dictator. However, I think something is happening, unlike the usual things we've seen before in American politics.

The Supreminati and/or Oligarch have been said to truly control everything: the Federal Reserve, music and movie industries, the media, the medical industry, farming, education, trade, and many other sectors that are essential to our everyday existence. This is their empire.

It will be impossible to ever return to or experience a free country, with a healthy middle class, until this group and the Federal Reserve are out of our lives. Picture the Monopoly™ board. These people own the Boardwalk and Park Place side of the board and more. The game is rigged against ordinary people. They control everything. They pay off Congress to legislate in favor of them retaining their absolute control. Politicians get money and live the life of the upper-class citizens while the masses get marginalized and crushed.

The U.S. Congress was supposed to be the body to protect the people from mischievous and dangerous acts by the president towards people, along with other functions they perform. It seems Congress has not protected the interests of the people, which makes it safe to assume they are bought off and under the control of these Oligarchs: The Supreminati. That, I imagine, is the way our country (and perhaps the world) has operated for centuries. These people are a significant threat to all humanity. For me, this is a bigger fight than racism. This group is out to destroy the soul of humanity. I view them as Satan's committee.

I also fear Trump can be bought off by The Supreminati. His love for money far outweighs his stand for righteousness. He strikes me as the type of guy who, if these powerful or wealthy families invite him to join, he would in a heartbeat. Look at his behavior. Isn't it clear he thinks he is a king?

White Supremacy is an ideology that manipulates politics and affects all matters in American society, with the sole objective being to lift white people above others and keeping blacks at the bottom (i.e.

(*keeping the white community pure*). There seems to be a distinction between The Supreminati and The Deep State. This group appears to be a more significant threat than White Supremacy. This group, I believe, is comprised of Satan's disciples, who are all white supremacists.

White people, in general, have never had a more transparent look at the ugliness of white supremacy than they do now under Trump's watch, which to me, is life-changing. I presume many whites can now see how cunning, treacherous, and evil some of their very own people are. Donald Trump is quite the lesson. The United States will never be the same. Will we pivot into something satanic and ugly, or will we move towards the divine greatness that lies in the potential of that which our foundation is laid?

While we are experiencing uproar, protests, lawlessness, and revolt during this transition, it is necessary. We must endure this turmoil. Change won't be easy; change never is. Although this may be the hardest change we have ever experienced in this country, truth will prevail. We will be, what we are meant to be. I pray the good from our human race will overwhelm and prevail over the evil and hatred Donald Trump has lifted.

The Supreminati vs. God

We are all part of God's human race. There is only one race in God's eyes, and it is His human race. God made the world full of colors, including humans and everything else in it. I suppose our white supremacist men and women should begin to ask for understanding as to why their hearts are so filled with the disease of hate for people who don't share their skin color or beliefs: Jews and especially black people.

How do you behave with such a hateful heart and claim homage to God? When you think about God and pray to Him, does your heart feel any love? If so, then do you not believe God loves black people also? How, then, does hate enter in? God is love; therefore, hate cannot come from Him and flow into people. Where, then, does hate come from? If you are filled with it, then who is really controlling you? How can you think its God? God is love. Do you agree God is love? If so, then please explain your hate, white supremacist. Are you honest with yourself? Even if you are lying to the world, are you honest with yourself?

America is appalling. The revolution, they've said, would not be televised. Well, thanks to social media, it is "social medialized." In case you didn't realize, the revolution is now. White people have already started shooting. How did this country get to such a horrible state? Who is really to blame for the poor quality of life shared by so many Americans, especially the poor and blacks?

The story that defines black life in America is not the pursuit of the American dream. Instead, it is the long and weary fight for fundamental human rights and privileges all human beings deserve to have in their lives. I guess pointing the finger at anyone specific would be hard to do, considering the many factors that go into manufacturing such a pervasive state of living.

I am asking we take a closer look at the families who own the Federal Reserve. They seem to get no blame for anything. I ask myself, "How can one be so powerful and control so much of our everyday living conditions and get no blame?" Existing under the radar is an understatement; this group is something special.

Digress with me for a moment. A $100 bill is printed and put into circulation, let's say in 1950. Every time that bill exchanges hands, it is taxed. That is interest paid simply to use this piece of paper as a fiat currency to trade for goods and services. Your bank gives you a $100 bill, which you use to buy groceries, and it's taxed. When the grocery stores use it to buy supplies, it's taxed. The supplier or wholesaler then uses it to pay for storage facilities, and it's taxed. The storage facility uses it to pay a janitorial service to clean its facility; it's also taxed. The janitorial services buy equipment; it's taxed again. That goes on and on. Here we are, 70 years later, and that single $100 bill has moved tens of thousands of times from one hand to another; and each time, it is taxed. Money that goes back to the Federal Reserve, who originally authorized the bill. What do we have here? I am only talking about one bill. How much tax money has this particular bill generated for the Federal Reserve cartel families in 70 years? In the world of finances, that is called a Ponzi scheme. How much do a million $100 bills generate in taxes?

Think about this; your paycheck is hijacked before you get it. I once read that one week's worth of earnings each month goes to the Federal Reserve families. Simply put, three to four months of every year you work, your earnings go to paying taxes. By the time we are 65 years of age, roughly 15 years of our life earnings would have been used for the payment of taxes! This information blew my mind, but it's real.

How can this group take no blame for the state of this country? Republicans will tell you it's President Obama's fault. He ran up trillions in debt. However, I always ask the questions of, "How do we know the amount that was really collected in taxes?"

Since no group regulates the Federal Reserve, there is no accounting for their books; they have never been audited. I am not the brightest guy when it comes to understanding these numbers, so help me understand, please. The US Treasury's relationship with the Federal Reserve leaves room for a lot of suspicious activity. Here is a piece I read. (http://www.usa-exile.org/news/0306/02/elitefedfamilies.html)

Who are These People?

The complete control of monetary policy (and money itself) in the United States does not lie in the hands of Congress or the people. The privately-held Federal Reserve Corporation owns, controls, and manipulates us.

What's even more amazing is that banks with foreign ties and ownership are included on the list of big banks that own and control the Federal Reserve. According to the General Accounting Office (GAO), 30% of U.S. banking assets were controlled by foreign interests in 2016 ($1.4 **trillion**). Write to your representatives in Washington, D.C., for the names of the top 20 institutions that received interest payments for our national debt since 1983, and you will see for yourself just who's in control and who we're paying hard-earned taxes to.

 J. W. McCallister, an oil industry insider with House of Saud connections, wrote in The Grim Reaper that information he acquired from Saudi bankers cited 80% ownership of the New York Federal Reserve Bank—by far the most powerful federal branch by just eight families; four of which reside in the U.S. They are the Goldman Sachs, Rockefellers, Lehman's, and Kuhn Loeb's of New York; the Rothschilds of Paris and London; the Warburg's of Hamburg; the Lazard's of Paris; and the Israel Moses Seifs of Rome. Here is the global Oligarchy.

I am intrigued by the mystique surrounding some of the organizations we hear about. For instance, the Rothchild's—the Bohemian Grove. The Bilderberg Group—Skull and Bones, the Council of Foreign

Relations, the Jesuits, the Vatican's, and the Zionist. These are some *very secret* organizations. Do some research on these groups. Notice you rarely hear any politician, news reporters, or anyone in the media talking about these groups and their influence over our lives. There is a reason for this. Why are these groups secretive, powerful, and feared? I have never seen an organization of benevolence enforce such secrecy about their doings, like the Red Cross or United Way.

The rule of The Supreminati and Oligarchy have dominated the world for thousands of years. In the carnal sense, there is no match for this wicked Supreminati group. The next encounter for them, is God. It must be. Because here on Earth, the only opponent for them would be if the people came together as one and fought as one to end the Federal Reserve and get them out of our lives first and foremost. That would take back our economy. They are not federal; they have absolutely nothing to do with the federal government. They are simply a private LLC or S-Corp that pulled off the biggest client in banking history; the USA—and the world.

Perhaps you are a Wells Fargo, Citi Bank, or Bank of America customer. America is their customer. The people need to come together to overthrow this Oligarchy, and it probably exceeds the impossible; they've made sure of it. We are divided and at war with each other in nearly every area or aspect of our lives, so I genuinely believe the next level for this powerful group of people is the Creator.

When I think of the way they've monopolized the money, resources and control that have impoverished countries—leaving children to die of starvation, famine, diseases and burdening the working class with the daily struggle to earn barely enough to provide a standard of living that leaves most people one check away from skid row—the passage in the Bible that reads "...it will be easier for a camel to make it through the eye of a needle than for the rich to get into heaven," begins to make more sense to me. This level of greed *must be the precursor to* biblical prophecy. I used to struggle with understanding the passage found in Mark 10:25. Now, when I look at the evil hand of The Supreminati, I get the picture.

Yeah, It's Like That

I am startled at how whites revere the founding fathers. What does it say having slave owners writing the Constitution, a document of laws and rights put in place to ensure order and righteousness among citizens and their government? To me, it is paradoxical, hypocritical, and just flat-out evil to have slaves serving you tea as you are writing the laws for a nation of people to live by—even laws that deem your tea servers to be three-fifths of a human being.

According to Loretta Ross, "Most white supremacists in America believe the United States is their 'Christian' nation, with a special relationship between religion and their rule of law. Because racists give themselves divine permission from God to hate, they often don't see their actions are driven by hate; they claim to 'just love God and the white race.'" (Loretta Ross. PRA)

Therefore, most racist whites really do not see themselves filled with hate; they really don't. Go on to YouTube and pull up the Ota Benga story.

In the early 1900s, white scientists literally forced a young black man into a habitat at the Bronx zoo with monkeys. This was done in their ridiculous quest to prove some evolutionary theory that blacks came from apes and to show the whole world whites are superior beings or "preferred" race. Ota Benga was eventually petitioned for and turned over to a black preacher in Virginia. Ota later committed suicide. The story says depression was the reason. (Wikipedia)

The belief system of white supremacists in America is reflected in this act, so to speak. Did they force themselves to believe God wanted them to be supreme above all others? Did they raise generation after generation of children, teaching and instilling this belief system into whites? Is this why they can inflict injustice without a conscious? Is this why they can just gun down a black man with 21 bullets and justify it by merely saying the kid posed a threat to them? Why don't we see many black officers being threatened in this way from black men? Is this why they could come together in a picnic-like setting to burn or hang a black child routinely as a ceremony, with their white children watching?

Think about a group of adults burning a black human child while justifying and preparing their children to behave accordingly. That is sickening. Can you honestly say this is not an act of the devil? To burn an innocent child alive? You can sit there and watch it, then tell your children it is the way some god meant for it to be?

In my own point of view, leaving the white children at home so they would not witness these devilish acts is one thing, but bringing them along to watch a murder is satanic. What is the effect today on white people to have this behavior burned into their psyche? Racism Anonymous is worth a shot; we should try it.

The devil is alive, and he is dwelling inside some people, acting out. Therefore, I say to even non-racist white people, it is worth making sure there is no residue left.

Are all men created equal? No matter what the skin color was, it's inconceivable that when people looked at a black man, he was mistaken for something less than a man made in God's image. The evidence in the history of black and white relations is clear and, without a doubt, horrific. It seems the cry from blacks has been a request for fairness and equality. Also, there's been a need for justice and equality. That means, to me, the real powers who run and manipulate our lives are not giving up the fairness and equality sought after by blacks. Think about it. Blacks have been asking, petitioning, begging, and marching for many decades.

I have never seen white supremacists looking inside themselves to own up to and admit the hate they feel inside is just evil. *Evil, for what reason?* I conclude it's the devil. Does any other race harbor hate for another culture like the hate whites have for blacks and Jews? Is the hatred for the Jews from the Germans as bad as what blacks have received from whites? I once was even asked if the extermination of Jewish people was worse than the life-long, ongoing, murder, and decimation of black people.

Understand, blacks will never give up on pleading for absolute equality. I don't think the supremacists will ever change either. It is what it is, but they will die off. I hate to sound pessimistic, but instead of trying to change The Supreminati, blacks must fix the problem that has conditioned us.

I do recognize and salute the many programs blacks have put together to help specific causes in our community. I honestly believe blacks have the power to repair the black family and society. Nonetheless, this current State of Black Life needs emergency-like attention. It cannot be gradual; it must be a shock-like treatment to blow the state of black life off its axis.

In the year 1700 (per Wikipedia), there were roughly 223,000 white people in the 13 colonies of the U.S. and approximately 27,000 blacks. Today, they report more than 220 million white citizens and around 40 million blacks. If the black population had grown at the same pace whites did, how many black people would be in this country? Imagine if the U.S. had more than 100 million black people in the country today, what would America look like? I guess they had to stop it, and they did.

I've racked my brain many times about the state of black people in this world. Somehow, it seems we were cursed here on earth. Look around the world; it looks like black people are in the worst conditions of all. The American dream is something like a myth. For black people, it's been a long and weary fight for fundamental human fairness everyone deserves to receive, and this fight has been ongoing for an exceptionally long time.

Maybe when Hip Hop becomes a senior citizen, and the old whites die off, then fairness to all may emerge into existence. If you are not clear on the true definition of White Supremacy, it means to keep white blood pure. It also means to keep everyone beneath whites and to destroy black men and Jews at all costs, in my opinion. What we need to understand is White Supremacy built America. Blacks didn't mix blood with whites. Whites, however, mixed with blacks for breeding purposes. How hypocritical is it to claim to hate blacks but be unable to resist sexing the beautiful curvy black women? They didn't breed black men and white women together.

I imagine many would agree there has been a movement to dumb down America. The office of the presidency is the exclamation point of this movement; the mission is complete. The highest office in the land now ultimately reflects this dumbing down. Don't get me wrong; I don't think Donald Trump is a dumb man. I think he is brilliant for the purposes of bad and not good. I believe he is not seasoned or studied enough to proficiently satisfy the task of the presidency. If George W. Bush was a "C" student in school, then Donald Trump cheated on all his tests and got a "C," his level of intelligence is not up to par with the position he was elected into.

Sadly enough, Trump seems to be ignorant about so many critical worldly matters. He is such a good bullshitter; he finagles his way through things. The weird thing is, if he is weakening The Deep State, then I am glad. If the people were able to measure pure qualification for the 2016 election in this way, it would clearly have demonstrated how lop-sided the candidates were as far as being qualified.

Let's use the position of an airplane pilot as a prop. Hillary is flying the Democratic plane, which is plane #1. Then, Donald Trump is flying the Republican plane, which is plane #2. If people were told to go and board the plane based on their confidence in the qualifications of the pilot, in my opinion, the entire nation would have boarded Hillary's plane—no matter how many criminal acts she was accused of committing. Trump's family probably wouldn't have gone with him either.

The Independent's, out of a heightened and uncontrollable state of being petrified, would have apologized to the Democrats. Putin, because of mixed messages by way of hacking, would have called for a truce with Hillary and asked Trump if he'd give her a ride. Trump, himself, while now forced to be honest about his own ability, would have unboarded the plane and said, "Obama bugged the plane."

I can finally say it seems Donald Trump represents the trueness of America's core personality. Think of all the racist things he said while running for office. Think about the belittling of women. Think of how much of a liar he has shown himself to be. Think of the character we have as the face of this country. Now think of the fact that he was elected into office as the president. Who was it that decided his presidency? Not the general public, Hilary had three million more votes. White Supremacy and the Electoral College is how he won. I'll just describe them as the group that regulates voting.

My understanding is of the original purposes of the Electoral College to prevent huge population states like Texas, New York, and California from overwhelming elections due to the vast number of people from just a few states, and the lack of political intelligence of common folks to be another reason, but power always corrupts. The flip-side is each state has two senators. Therefore, states like North and South Dakota, with a combined population of fewer than two million people, produces four senators, versus a state like California (with more than 30 million people) that only produces two senators. Go figure!

It appears to me Trump is not intellectually prepared to hold the position of the president. He seems to lack the compassion and humility to empathize with people unlike him; he also appears to not have the fundamental honesty it takes to gain other people's trust. Most of all, he lacks the wisdom and humility that comes from God, in my opinion.

What's ridiculously sad is Trump dragged the elections down to the lowest and most distasteful form of communication humans exercise. It was like an indignant-ass fool arguing. That was the language he was most comfortable with during the primaries up to the general election. Dirty, and disrespectful foul language was what he turned every debate into. *He Jerry Springer'd the elections.* That was the most comfortable form of communication for this candidate. Think about his base, the millions of white people who say "yeah" and cheer him up at his rallies. They favored the Jerry Springer like signifying. What does that say about them? It's sad to say, but that's the fiber that built America, and thanks to Trump, they all came out and stood proudly.

Why Do You Hate Blacks?

I get upset sometimes. Most white people speak as if blacks are always over-exaggerating the *daily racist encounters* they experience. Can you imagine being accused and convicted of the world's ugliest crime, as far as I am concerned? Spending six years of your life treated so inhumanely that you begin to believe you are not a beautiful human being, created by God, breaks your spirit. You become empty inside; it feels like you are dead.

I had begun to wonder if I was a sacrificial lamb or something, like Job in the Bible. I knew despite what the system was doing to me, God knew what happened. I just couldn't understand how He could allow such a thing to happen to me.

Consequently, I held onto the hope that God would be the final judge to all of it. If I didn't believe in God, I probably would have gone off the deep end somehow. I just couldn't accept He would never step in and do something.

Today, nearly 37 years later, I've been shaped and terribly affected by that incident; however, I always think about the lady who was the victim. She was from Hobart, Indiana, if I recall. I'd wonder at times how this event affected her. I also wonder if she feels anything about me spending six years of my life in prison. Despite what the court's conclusions were, only she, Pooney, God, and I know what happened that night.

Another thing I wonder is what does she say (if and when) she speaks to God about that ordeal, mainly about me spending six years of my life in prison for a crime against her. Could you witness a person going into incarceration for a crime committed against you, when deep in your heart, you know that person isn't guilty? Well, after 62 years, Carolyn Bryant confessed she fabricated the story about Emmet Till in a book by Timothy Tyson entitled: *The Blood of Emmet Till,* and I am an ex-felon now, with two strikes on my back (thanks to our justice system). These convictions have categorized me my entire life.

The police have been the bane of my existence. Sometimes I wonder if I should hate them, or should I hate both the police and the so-called American justice system both? I have been labeled with a description that in no way represents or describes who I am. Admittedly, I am no saint; I have engaged in some petty stealing as a teenager, so I cannot lie to God. However, this country has done a destructive job on my image. If you were me, would you hate the police and the American justice system? You don't need to answer that now; explain later.

I was 18 years old when this tragedy happened. The

shame and fear I initially felt were almost too much to bear. I couldn't believe I was in prison for such a horrible crime. I was particularly young at the time, and although I had committed my share of petty thefts, I had never been in jail before. That was some big-time shit. Fear went straight through my mind. You see, I had heard of what happens to people who go to prison for sexual offenses, but I didn't know what to expect. One night, I was in my neighborhood doing dumb shit; the next night, I was in what seemed to be hell-on-earth.

Culture shock doesn't even begin to describe what I experienced. It was a real fucking nightmare; I was traumatized, but not for fear of being in prison. I knew I had to survive and was prepared to die or kill for my life. I was traumatized because the transition from freedom to prison was so sudden. I went from hanging out with my homies, smoking weed, and playing the dozens in the hood, to the penitentiary, and it seemed to have happened overnight.

The year was 1983 B.C.—before crack. Picture Ice Cube and Chris Tucker in the movie *Friday*. Take out the threat of gun violence and crack, and this is where I was coming from. Then voila!

I was walking down a gallery of Menard Correctional Facility in Illinois, a maximum-security prison, listening to the voices of murderers, rapists, armed robbers, arsonists, and some of the most heinous criminals you can ever imagine, listening to the dialog of men who were serving life sentences, 200 years, 50 years, and everything in between. I was 19 years old and had no gang affiliation. I went from an aspiring athlete in high school to a prisoner in a maximum-security prison where serial killers like John Wayne Gacy are in.

Life was flashing before me daily. If someone came to harm me, I was going to try my best to kill such a person, so I walked really softly in that place. I was like a church mouse in maximum security who wanted to get out someday. Many of those people were never going to leave, and I tell you, you don't ever want to be living with people who have no hope for their future. They really don't give a fuck.

Living on the edge every day wasn't natural. Even now, I would rather die instantly than go back to prison to serve major time and die slowly in a vortex of pain, anger, and a pervasive desire for revenge.

White Friends,
You're Really Sick Too

I hope the day is extremely near when many blacks come to the end of their rope of only complaining about conditions for African-Americans in this country. (The way I see it.) America is the architect of the conditions in black communities. Why would America reach out to help? It deliberately created it. I will never completely give up on things changing, but America deliberately created this mess.

While I am sold on the fact that White Supremacy will continue its course, I hope many ordinary whites will understand racism and hatred were taught and instilled in them. They can now do something to try and heal themselves of this ugly, horrific disease, and maybe fight to overthrow the supremacy keeping this disease alive. Racism Anonymous is a great idea!

As strange as this may sound, racism is possibly the worst disease on Earth. It's rooted in hate, and every ill we live with is directly or indirectly akin to it. Greed, gluttony, selfishness revenge, etc., are all diseases of the heart. When love is absent, all these things manifest.

Hip Hop is kryptonite to racism. Fast forward 100 years, and Hip Hop might be the dominant reason why all the racial divides get erased. The young white kids today will eventually become leaders in politics and corporations tomorrow. They are not racists. You can't be down with Hip Hop and be a total racist; it's almost impossible. Just maybe a change has come.

When I listen to some whites speak in the media, it's a shame many do not see themselves as racists.

They have become so entitled and accustomed to their built-in privilege that some wouldn't dare consider changing anything that truly evens the playing field for other people. They are incredibly self-righteous. They believe the laws and standards set in this country are the way things should remain. They do not consider the fact that this country has a massive influx of Asians, Chinese, Latinos, and West Indians, in addition to blacks from Africa, Jamaica, Cuba, Bahamas, Belize, and South America. Today, the complexion of this country is not the same as yesterday, yet the land still maintains most of the law and order written by and in the interests of white Supremacy.

Look at the Tea Party and other white groups. Haven't you heard them say things like, "We have lost our country?" They are serious about the U.S. being theirs, just like your house is your house. Can you allow someone to stay in your home and then allow them to change the rules in your house? That

is how the extreme whites feel about this country—
that they literally stole from Native Americans.

White Supreminati took it upon themselves to birth
and deliver one of the sickest and wickedest evils in
this country, maybe on this earth: racism. In my
opinion, it is the eighth-most deadly sin. I wonder if
they created this xenophobia themselves, or if it's
Satan working through them to exterminate the
black man from God's creation? That could be the
only explanation as to why some of them don't see
themselves as racists, but it could also be a spiritual
attack on God's children.

Although blacks have suffered tremendously in the
hands of White Supremacy, from a spiritual
standpoint, in my opinion, whites need more
healing than blacks do. Think of how sick it is to
declare another human being only three-fifths
human, then write this into your nation's
constitution, and then teach this to your children for
centuries. Didn't anyone in the room realize

something was wrong?

Many of the racial teachings were done under the guise of Christianity. I hope white people will someday realize and address that many of them come from an extraordinarily sick and wicked pedigree. Their sickness needs treatment and healing. Racism Anonymous would be a great platform to get this healing.

I realize all whites didn't agree with Hitler, but most of them were here in this nation, as White Supremacy influenced its development. Many of them went along for the ride and reaped the benefits of built-in "affirmative action" and white privilege. Much wealth was amassed through the cotton industry by many ordinary white families. This wealth disparity affects generations. It cannot fix itself, so there is accountability for regular whites to some degree.

While the great-great-grandchildren of many white

families are born into a family legacy of success or some degree of stability, today, many great-great-grandchildren of black families are born into broken, fatherlessness, and poverty with little degree (if any) of security.

To sum it up, the state of the nation's economy and its labor force did not come together by chance. It was mostly by design, inconspicuously conceived to oppress the black man and black woman by extinction of the black community.

You're Doing Us

I do not see much love and respect in the black community anymore. The black family seems thoroughly diluted with each generation seemingly independent of the previous one. The strength and bonds that should connect the offspring do not seem to be present anymore. The love that passes down the family tree is no longer available. It's evident there is little love in the city, the family, and the black community at large.

What happened to the black family? There is a crisis of unprecedented magnitude in the black community, one that goes to the very heart of its survival. The black family and community are failing. The absence of fathers is the bane of it, predisposing black children (boys especially, but increasingly girls as well) to fail in primary areas of their lives. That sets the stage for economic hardship, which then progresses to the many things wrong in our communities. Criminal behavior then kicks in and onto an *intergenerational repetition* of this ugly grim cycle.

When did fathers ideally start to fall off from black families? I am not entirely sure, but it seems the 1950s and 1960s weren't as bad as the 1970s and 1980s. As time elapsed, it got worse. In the year 2015, according to government statistics, 72% of African-American children were born to unmarried mothers (*the root.com*). The article goes on to list various reasons why these numbers are the way they are, including the residual effects of slavery, segregation, and the penal system. The incarceration rate for African-Americans was then six times the national average. While many blacks would argue there is a horrible conspiracy going on when it comes to incarcerating black men, I have a more profound concern as I look at a sneaky reality taking place in our society.

The U.S. economy was devastated by the outsourcing of millions of labor jobs to foreign countries. Lower tax rates and cheap labor made it a smart business for numerous companies to send many of our service, tech, and factory jobs overseas. I try to imagine the total number of positions that left the U.S. I've heard numbers as high as eight million. Many of these jobs may never return, which makes it exceedingly difficult for many black men to find decent employment to provide for their families. I am speaking of the many non-degree-carrying black men who are left without a stable career that usually follows getting a good education.

Years ago, CNBC aired a special entitled, *"Billions Behind Bars."* The show centered on the privatization of the prison industry, which has resulted in prisoners making many products, including jeans, waterbeds, floor tile, motorcycle parts, vineyards, goat farms, components for Patriot missiles, and tilapia fish sold out of Whole Foods stores. When you think about it, preparing prisoners with a skill to help them when they re-enter society is a good thing, but is reforming prisoners the real inspiration behind this act, or has global outsourcing gotten even cheaper? Should we call it prison-sourcing?

The average wage for a prisoner is about 50 cents per day. Think about it. Companies can hire 1,000 prisoners to do eight hours of work, and it would cost only $4,000 in labor in exchange for 8,000 hours of man labor. Prisoners are motivated to work, which keeps them busy as their days pass faster. Employers are also guaranteed excellent attendance from prison-bound employees. The company isn't even required to pay the workman's compensation insurance. That looks like slavery to me.

I could probably buy into this as an act to

rehabilitate prisoners if there were good factory jobs in our communities that benefit from such labor skills. What is a prisoner supposed to do for employment when he/she is released? Move to another country? Many factories have gone overseas, and robots are here. Instead of producing all those products in factories where U.S. citizens can have jobs and strengthen the U.S. economy, someone decided it is more valuable to generate these products in prisons across America. That is a form of *legalized slavery*.

The 13th Amendment to the United States Constitution outlawed slavery and involuntary servitude, *except* as a punishment for a crime. It implicitly states, 'once convicted of a crime.' That means this form of slavery is constitutional, but maybe it's just a pure coincidence that black men represent nearly 50% of the prison population and 90% of the cheap labor force working behind bars.

Blacks are accused heavily of exaggerating racism.

Look at what's going on with the marches against police officers killing unarmed blacks. We have been accused of always playing the race card. What amazes me is that whites act as if they have not been stricken heavily with the disease of racism. They act as if they are over it now or have healed. The problem with this is whites cannot show one act in history that demonstrates their efforts to treat or heal themselves of the disease of racism. Like any illness, it needs treatment. This illness is a generational thing; it has been passed down through centuries. Can you name one program in history designed for white people to deal with their very own sickness? Is racism the only illness on the earth that doesn't need treatment or healing?

Personally, I don't think many white people (as a whole) clearly understand the depth of their problem. It is entwined wickedly in their fiber. If the problem wasn't real, then many blacks probably wouldn't still be addressing it daily. Still, it is a bad problem inside many white Americans. I'm not only talking about white supremacists, hate groups, and terrorist groups like the Klan. I'm talking about many of your average ordinary white Americans. Remember when the guy, Michael Richards, who plays Kramer from *Seinfeld*, got in trouble for speaking negatively about blacks? I really like the guy as a comedic actor, but deep down, I never knew what he harbored in his heart and mind.

Al-Qaeda, Isis, and other terrorist groups from the Middle East are treated as Americas most wanted. But the KKK, a white terrorist group, and white hate groups are free to operate and function in the U.S. Why can't our government wipe them off the earth, too? Why are they permitted to operate right here in the U.S.? If it were ISIS marching in Charlottesville, what would our government have done to them? Why is this country home for the KKK? How can whites think they are free of racism if they can live right beside a terrorist group like the

KKK, who are known to kill, murder, and hang innocent black people? This is a hate group, isn't it?

What is the difference between the so-called ISIS and Al-Qaeda's terrorist attacks and hate against America, and the KKK's terrorist attacks and hate against black people? Is America saying hate from White Supremacy is okay in this country? That it is an official legal entity in the U.S.?

The KKK is a white terrorist organization. The Aryan Nation, the Skinheads, the National Alliance, and the Church of the Creator are growing in numbers and influence. Swastikas and Uzis are replacing hoods and crosses. What does that make our government? Our law enforcement? Our politicians who vote heavily for wars to fight terrorists? If they allow these organizations or groups to exist with an agenda of killing and destroying black people, then what are these agencies really saying? A terrorist group that kills black people is welcome? I guess killing because of skin color is acceptable in America. If ISIS was killing only black people, would America give them a pass?

I am not saying every white person is racist. I personally have a few great white friends. Barry Elrod is like my brother, so much so, he gets on my damn nerves sometimes. Heidi Plonski, one of my best friends (white or otherwise) in the world, has such a beautiful heart, and there isn't a racist bone in her body.

A British imperialistic ideology, White Supremacy, was the prevailing mindset during the founding of this country. It is woven into the fabric of the New World. Many of the successors of the Founding Fathers who later wore those ugly-hooded sheets, where are they now? I believe they are scattered in the government parastatals, political parties, banks, media, and other influential areas of this country, still maintaining their creed of White Supremacy, though some of them have removed the ugly-hooded sheets. Sadly for blacks, they have blended in with the non-racist ordinary white people. I make these points because racism is deeply rooted into the hierarchy of this country.

The Obama hate machine was not surprising to me. Countless times, I have worked in management positions where I experienced a microcosm of that exact hate from whites. It was shocking how vicious the hate was; at times, I couldn't believe it. It came from people I had never done anything wrong to, and some I had never laid my eyes on. The mere fact that I was considered the best at sales, management, and sales trainer unleashed an unbelievable amount of hatred towards me from white people. They just couldn't take it; it's ironic.

Things were merely fine up until the moment I took a position as their superior or their leader. Then, their true colors surfaced. I am willing to bet every black man who has ever held a superior position over whites in America can tell a similar story.

Undoubtedly, black women can relate to this, as well. Because of it, the time is **now** for black men and black women to re-approach their relationships. We must fix our broken "black love" for each other. I missed receiving the love of my mother, sister, grandmother, and grandfather. It's sad and horrible what White Supremacy has done to our people.

When I look at my life, I can connect most things in it directly or indirectly to the root, or the foundation, and the pedigree I come from. I don't present this to imply we are all bound by generational blessings or curses. I have seen numerous stories of people who have managed to extricate themselves from characteristics and behaviors passed down from their family tree. However, more than that, I have seen masses of blacks to be an extension of broken and disconnected families. This behavior has become like a snowball rolling downhill or consumed in an avalanche. It has moved *beyond the crisis stage*. It has reshaped and defined an entire group of people with a nearly uncontrollable momentum. This momentum must be stopped, or the black community will be stuck in a permanent and detrimental devolution that will become as natural as the sun rising or the grass growing, and it will take a powerful phenomenon to stop it.

Black people are not multiplying fruitfully. To me, it seems blacks are repelling against each other. This deficiency is taking place at the core of both the black male and female. Why is this union not functioning in a way that is healthy and conducive to building a family? Why has it become so difficult for black men and women to love each other like other cultures love and develop their own generations with strength and security?

My mother was a single parent for all my life. I was the last of four children; my older three siblings were from her previous marriage. To my recollection, neither of our dads were true fathers to their children. To this day, I struggle to forgive the man who impregnated my mother with me. He didn't father me as *his* child; he was a no-show, which is terrible.

I wonder if my birth father was just another casualty of this avalanche, or was he just an irresponsible man. Sometimes, men abandon their babies for different reasons. Still, it's a shame. I look around and see many blacks who have had this same experience. That seems to be a norm within the black community. Statistics show a single parent, the mother, raises 70% of black children.

The funny thing is, I genuinely don't believe black men are naturally irresponsible. Abandoning their responsibility of fatherhood in such massive numbers seems so unnatural. It doesn't make sense in the natural realm of things; just look at other ethnicities of men—they are not like this. To me, this is the evidence that this situation is not natural or normal but deserves immediate attention. However, to me, it is based on the financial hardship imposed on the black male figure. Of course, other topical problems pronounce themselves, but social engineering is the primary cause of fatherless households and black men abandoning their children in my opinion. I know this behavior of blacks is engineered and manufactured. I will set out to prove this is factual; it is not my discovery. Many blacks have trumpeted this and lived with it for years.

I have heard many prominent blacks speak on this issue/subject; therefore, what I hope to do here is firmly press the reality that we must *shock the present state of black life off its current axis* and give way to a rebirth that blacks can come together as a group and put the community into its own sustainable action. I also want to remind us of *Black Wall Street* to offer some fuel to get back to establishing a similar economy of our own. Additionally, I want to offer some ideas on mending the relationship between black men and black women, which is the most challenging task of all.

I want to point out another interesting fact: many black women have seemingly decided *against* being a parent. Nationwide reports indicate that since 1970, more than 13,000,000 black babies have been aborted. (http://www.blackgenocide.org)

This number blows me away. Think about the number of black lives that could have spawned from this 13,000,000—possibly, at least five to ten times more blacks would have been in this country! The black population could have been more than 100 million here in the United States. What would that be like? (A scary thought to white supremacists, no doubt.) Why has it not grown past 13% of the population? The question is simply: Why are so many black women having abortions? Why are so many black women left to raise children by themselves? Why does it seem like this problem is not as prevalent in other ethnicities of people?

I look at my immediate family's situation, and I tell you we were very disconnected. Yes, we are all blood-related, but we did not bond or unify in a way a family is supposed to bond, love, and support each other. Parental influence was absent; the glue was missing, which was like a missing piece. It was not my mother's fault. She alone worked two jobs trying to support four kids. With eight hours of sleep needed each day, how much time is left to be a parent? God bless her endless efforts, support, and care. She may have worked herself to death.

I see this to be common with many black women. I was a teenager when my mother passed. Afterward, my siblings and I didn't do things together much as a family; everyone was living their own life. Each person was consumed completely, trying to make ends meet. Poverty has its way of doing this to people.

I reflect on some of the simple things families should do, like having dinner together at the dinner table. I cannot remember a time in my life where I had a simple birthday party. I can't even remember a time in my life when I sat at the table and had dinner with my entire family. Is this normal for black families? I'm not sure, but it seems like I missed something.

When I see big families on television eating together, it looks like a bond is occurring that is incomparable to anything I witnessed as a child or teen. It seems to solidify a family in such a unique way. What I mean is, the *entire family*. Sure, I can remember sitting at the table with only my brother across it, but what I mean is a full family, and this lack is at the heart of the storyline here. What happened to healthy black families?

I came to learn my mother's immediate family behaved almost the exact way my family did. My late aunt, Lauretta, was best friends with my mother. She would tell me my maternal grandfather's family was disconnected in the same way. That helped me understand how things pass from generation to generation. Just when I was beginning to think it was all about me, it became more apparent that a great deal of what I am today passed down to me from previous generations. It's like the life God gave to me came with a link to some group's history. That is interesting because when I look around at other people, I sometimes visualize the history they're linked to. It's like I can almost tell if history is like a ball and chain attached to the ankle, or if that history is like a wind that fuels their wings. Presently, it seems vividly clear to me.

I have many nieces and nephews who appear to be having the exact type of experience of a disconnected family. Strangely, I feel I have personally become one of the realities of life in the history that members of my family are linked to. I am unhappy to be passing along this same history of disconnection given to me, but it's like an avalanche I can't seem to stop. I can see it, though, and it just keeps going from generation to generation. It's a sure bet that unless there is a shift, the children of the next generation will experience the same disconnection, which is incredibly sad.

The major cause of this disconnection is the problems stemming from the relationships between the black man and the black woman. This union needs to be much stronger. The black man has become the most damaged link in this equation. This weakness is partially a maturation issue but is mainly due to social engineering and a deliberate attack on black men. The most devastating side effect of this is an economic weakness, which stems from the lack of proper conditioning which, for the most part, can only be passed down by a father.

The sisters have done better than the brothers. Most of our sisters had mothers than our brothers had fathers. That is the cause of what presents the imbalance to the black woman's life. That is the first link broken and causing the entire black community to be in shambles. It is kind of like a chain on a bicycle, in that all the little stubs are no longer held together. They exist, but they are not linked.

The very first stub in the link is the black man and the black woman together as one. If the first link (black man and woman) was bonded as one, then one could link adequately and attach the rest of the links. That would then create the strength and leverage for the remaining ones to connect and hold fast, but be flexible.

The rest of the links represent the black family. Since the first link is broken, the remaining links cannot find enough support to realize their proper formation. If only the first link could be repaired, I know the black family would begin to heal and perform the way it should. Then the black community's structure would improve and prosper.

Have you ever fixed your bike and began riding it again? It was a good feeling, wasn't it? It's going to be much harder to repair the relationship between the black man and the black woman; still, black people should begin immediately to improve their relationships, especially within the family. It may be the only way on earth to repair the damages of the African-American family and people here in the United States. That could be the path to getting the black community healthy again.

The black man has suffered the greatest damage in this link/chain analogy; he must be rebuilt first. He is *10 times* more damaged than the black woman. The way the black man has been weakened makes him almost impossible to repair, but it must be done. A masterfully-executed series of inconspicuous and cunning strategies have broken the brothers down. There must be a laser-focused and deliberate approach to fixing this broken part.

I know many black people have become frustrated. Fixing this crisis between the black man and black woman cannot be left to chance. The technique that has broken this relationship is so cunning, it is almost invisible. I compare it with living unknowingly with a deadly disease or having mold in your house. The problem is almost undetectable; it is hidden somewhere under the layers of black characteristics and personalities. The naked eye cannot see it; it's cunning.

Although the black man has suffered the greatest damage, this cunning virus has a dual counterpart that birthed and lived inside the black woman. Each day, these counterparts work unknowingly against each other, like two magnets that want to come together, but they just keep repelling and fighting.

The media, in general, and television, in particular, uses imagery and deception to continually fuel the separation of black men and women. Black Entertainment Television (BET), I wish it remained under black ownership. It could have been used in ways that would project better imagery for black youth.

The deliberate strategy imposed to separate the black man and the black woman has taken up permanent residence inside the behavior of many black individuals. It presents itself as a deadly disease that is detrimental and slowly killed the harmonious relationship between them. It was a masterplan, executed so well it has sustained its purpose and impact for centuries now. The evidence of its success is the broken black family and (ultimately) the stymied black race. This problem cannot fix itself, nor can time alone heal it. The way this problem is designed, time is like a steroid to it. Time will only enhance it while fueling it to grow bigger. A strategy must be mapped out to throw this crisis off course.

I have a suggestion. It seems to me this country is in a near class war; the black community should run back to its corners to fix the black race. The hate is not only deep; it's cunning.

African-American Genesis

Black men and women need to re-shift the axis. Blacks have been stuck in this terrible cycle of what I call *non-fruitful reproduction* and cannot seem to shake it. According to the self-proclaimed author of black-on-black self-destruction (Willie Lynch), black people will continue damaging themselves for an exceedingly long time. In his words, "We [meaning white people and slave owners] have created an orbiting cycle that turns on its own axis forever."

Black men and women need to have a phenomenon of its own take place. Lynch says, without a phenomenon, the existing state of destructive Negro (black) life may last for hundreds or even thousands of years. If only blacks could press the restart button and get off on a different foot. Maybe slacks could then build and support their families like other groups do, providing the next generation of blacks a good foundation or family legacy to come into when they are born. That is how it should be.

Unfortunately, blacks cannot simply press the restart button, just like we mature from a teenager to a middle-aged or elderly adult and cannot press restart to be a teenager again. Our behavior, practices, and conditioning mature as well, and this makes it nearly impossible to rewind and redo them. They become a permanent characteristic that defines people, ultimately shaping the entire culture.

What is interesting is these characteristics can be absolutely good or intrinsically bad. That is the prevalent key. It's like the ingredients that go into baking a cake. You can mess up the cake or make a great one. Look at the elements that created the behavior and practices of black people in this country. If you read the ingredients section on the side of the box, one would probably agree blacks did not get the good stuff. The ingredients are horrifying—intentionally horrifying. Blacks can change things, though, which would be much better than allowing things to remain as they are and 10 times better than expecting that one day, the government or Supreminati will apologize for some of the dreadful acts committed against black people.

Since black people make up roughly 13% of the American population, 40–50 million people today, then how is it that since slavery, the black community has grown so little? There are guesstimates that the combined numbers of total slaves brought over in the Trans-Atlantic Slave Trade (beginning in the mid-1500s) were at least 50 million imported slaves. I even heard numbers as high as 100 million because slaves were shipped continuously through the 1800s. Let's say the actual number was 40 million. We probably cannot be sure, but let's go with it nonetheless. (Even that is probably on the low side.)

If the slave trade started in the mid-1500s, then five centuries later, in 2020, the number 40 million has only grown to 40-50 million black people in this country today. Given this scenario, it appears the population growth of black people has been halted. My gut feeling is it is much worse. I presume the number of slaves brought over was much higher than 40 million, but the point I am making is not about the number of slaves brought. It's more about the managing of these numbers since their abduction. In addition, the abortion-to-pregnancy ratio reveals there are 44 abortions for every one hundred pregnancies in the black community (http://www.blackgenocide.org/black.html).

Many black adults will echo this dilemma regarding the lack of good loving black relationships and broken homes in black communities. It is common knowledge the black family gets torn apart. Minister Farrakhan has delivered this message for decades. I believe there is nothing on earth better to a black man, except the love of God, than the love of a black woman. I also believe visa-versa. At the core, the brothers love the sisters, and the sisters love the brothers. It must be because it is *natural* and *pure*. As to my viewpoint, blacks are struggling to operate from the core. So many layers of (pardon my expression) "shit" have been stacked on that blacks are dysfunctional and cannot work from a core essence—sisters strong, brothers weakened. Black girls rock; black men get shot.

As mentioned earlier, this is old news. I have heard many speak on the existence of this dilemma with black men and black women; many black scholars and historians have written extensively on this matter. I personally am neither a scholar nor a historian. My educational qualification is just two associate degrees from a small college. However, my experiences are real, and my best qualification is the education of life written in my journey.

I know many would agree any dysfunction must be dealt with, treated, or healed to function correctly again. I am certainly not smart enough to figure out this solution, but thank God, when the dysfunction was created, *a mention of a solution to correct it was given at the same time.*

I am amazed at how apparent the cause of this dysfunction is. This difficult thing has behaved like an AIDS virus or something. It has taken over how black men and women behave towards each other. It has altered the growth and development of black relationships, which affects the development of the *intra*-racial family in consequence. I am saddened at how difficult the implementation of a worthy solution has been.

There are many single professional and educated black women out there. This void has been a problem for an awfully long time for them. I've noticed black women, between the 1950s and 1980s, especially seem to have experienced this shortage of qualified black men.

Black women are graduating from college at an alarming rate than black men. Black men are dropping out of high school at an equally alarming rate. Why is this occurring? This information seems to indicate black men and women are moving socially and economically in opposite directions.

The divorce rate is off the chart, too. I've heard black women say, "There's a shortage of *qualified* black men." Many people state, "Black men are all lazy and trifling. Black men are this and that." I've read about sisters who don't date black men and visa-versa. I hear and see black men that say sisters are hard to deal with, and sisters are angry all the time, etc. Are blacks just dealing with a matter of not getting along, or are there other reasons causing this? This matter should be addressed carefully.

Hopefully, enough blacks care about the race as a whole. Like the Jewish people care for their brothers and sisters.

I see many brothers near and around my age (56) who, instead of being a mate to one of the many successful college-educated professional sisters (who are employed in white-collar professional careers and claim there aren't enough good qualified black men to complete them), are barely making it. Some of the brothers may have a job if they're lucky, but it's not a career. They are not equally yoked with the sisters. There's an imbalance—a career imbalance—that leads to a *self-worth* imbalance.

For some reason, the round peg is not fitting into the round hole. The brothers are completely different from the sisters in this land. Their paths are different. Brothers are still alive, and it seems they should align perfectly with the sisters, but somehow, their travels and journeys through life did not progress on similar tracks. The brothers seem to have been derailed somehow. The brothers' voyage got separated from the sisters' journey.

It seems the paths were separated right after high school, and many sisters went on to prepare for their careers, along with the idea of building a family, trying to keep with tradition. At the same time, many brothers got derailed from focusing on building a family and a stable, satisfying career. Somehow, distractions took over the brothers. It seems this is the critical time that a disconnection from the sisters took over.

Can I Just Be a Kid?

The Supreminati did a terrible job on the black family and community. They have not done anything to apologize or fix it, and I wonder if they ever will. Although reparations would show an attempt of accountability, it would not fix the problem. I am not talking about the apparent hell black people have endured from slavery in this country; I am talking about the cunning and inconspicuous damages that live on long after slavery. These damages are like a mole in an old building; they have been hidden cleverly in our behavior. It is psychological behavior modification.

These damages are more destructive because they are permanent ills that are tough to pinpoint, which makes the losses nearly impossible to fight off. You cannot fight an enemy you cannot see. The culprit has almost vanished. The spoils of the culprit are the only evidence that shows it ever existed, and those spoils were left in the psyche and behavior of black people.

The devastating acts of racism committed against me have steered my life into a dimension I could never have dreamt of. These acts have labeled me for life. They have tarnished my entire being and classified me into a group society views as detrimental and horrendous. These acts have shaped my views immensely. I now see the cunning way, devious pattern, and true manner in which The Supreminati operated; brilliantly and cunningly to destroy the black community. Thus, ultimately leading to the destruction of the entire black race.

I often think about how I've been shaped throughout life. In my efforts to climb the stratification ladder, I've spent most of my adult years trying to be accepted into so-called white Corporate America. I guess I bought into that three-fifths human thing put into the original Constitution subconsciously. The media reinforced this through "tell a vision" programming or TV, radio, and every other medium of communication in America. It seems I was reminded of it each time I attempted to take a step on that corporate ladder.

In my experiences, to gain real access to the high ranking or well-paying powerful corporate positions, one must be accepted and well-liked by whites. Being good at your craft or profession isn't enough. I find it difficult to be liked by whites. Evidently, they find it challenging to like me. I cannot think of any other reasons I would so need to be accepted by whites. Possibly, I've been stuck in this land of America too long. I've never worked to be approved by Latinos or Chinese people in the same way I have worked to be approved by whites.

At age 56, I feel a consistent series of race-centric

adversities in my life has tarnished me. I remember when I was a kid dreaming about the many things I could do when I grew up. My first love was to play basketball. Man, I loved to hoop. Like most kids, I was full of desire, determination, hope, and optimism. I had a raw zest for life and its possibilities. My soul and spirit were merely young and not yet worn by the heavy events of life. My thoughts presented me with an idea of fun with a great deal of enthusiasm and confidence that knew no boundaries. It seems like just yesterday, I had those thoughts, but years have passed since those positive ideas were desires within.

I'm different now. I'm all grown up, I think. These events, lessons, and experiences that life's given to me have done a significant job on my mind, heart, and spirit. Life has its way of coloring your heart. It is like a crayon box, and you never know which combination of colors will be used. If each color represented a life event, then what series of events or combinations of colors would end up coloring you or your life's biography? You never know if all bright colors or all dark colors will make up your life. Often, it turns out to be a combination of both. It makes me think of when I was just a baby. It's almost like I can remember when the very first crayon was taken out of the box. It may sound strange, but I can literally remember when the canvas was clean with no colors on it yet—when none of life's adversities or events had left its mark.

I wasn't prepared to deal with hate from whites. I especially was not ready to deal with hostility from my very own black people. It wasn't until high school when I met racism. I went to an interracial school called Bloom Trail. During my 1978 freshman year, there was a race riot. Before this, I had never really met racism because my neighborhood was all black. High school was the first time I encountered hate like that. The race riots were not bad in retrospect. However, I wouldn't consider it a full-blown race riot. There were spotty incidents throughout the school.

What sticks with me most from my high school days is a racial scenario around our football team. We had a phenomenal team. As eighth-graders, my team had a record of eight wins and zero losses. We won the conference title. As freshmen, we were eight and one, and as sophomores, we were eight and one. Over three years, we were 24 and two as a football team.

That was the class of 1982. We mixed in with the seniors during our junior year, and we were merely a below-average team. When we were coming into our senior year, there was a coaching vacancy. The previous varsity coach, Coach Velasquez had taken a job at another school. The entire football team, whites and blacks, petitioned to have our sophomore head coach, Ernie Turner be our head coach at the varsity level. We had a legitimate chance to be champs. We dominated on the field, and we didn't believe a team out there could stop us.

To our dismay, they didn't give Coach Turner the job. They gave it to Coach Tong, a white man who was not even a football coach. He was an assistant freshman wrestling coach and was relatively new to the school. Coach Lynn Motta, his assistant coach, actually ended up running the team. Lynn Motta was Coach Turner's assistant when we were sophomores. Do you remember *Remember the Titans* with Denzel Washington? My story is remarkably like the Titans' story. We were trailblazers. After the new coaching staff was hired, we had a terrible season and ended with only three wins.

I remember Coach Motta stealing our spirit from us. He actually ran the team. Immediately, he put a young white boy as the starting quarterback in front of another guy by the name of Tony Bell and me. He brought the white boy up as a sophomore to start in front of the two seniors, who were perhaps the leading two contributors to the previous year's record of 24 and 2.

On our way to the games, we used to sing on the bus to fire ourselves up. That had been our tradition since eighth grade. When we walked onto the opponent's field, they were already "shook" because we would be singing in unison like a Navy Seal squad that owned them already. Coach Motta stopped our singing and didn't let us do this in our senior year. In retrospect, it was a deeply sad injustice for the black seniors in my class. How many times does a young black man get an opportunity to play as a senior champion on a possible championship team, only to have his once-in-a-lifetime moment of being a senior in high school dampened because of a racist white coach running the team? How many black men across the U.S. can relate a similar story to mine?

To this day, I have a terrible dislike for Coach Motta. It is not just because of the football thing. You see, he failed me in his science class in hopes that it would lower my GPA and prevent me from playing football in my senior year. Despite his efforts, I passed his class. At the end of the semester, when we got our final grades, I received a "C" in his class, but by the time the grades came out on my report card, it showed an "F." I confronted him in a rage, but nothing changed.

I remember telling Coach Turner because he knew Motta didn't like me. Turner was a black teacher and coach. I guess there was nothing he could do. I sometimes wonder why Coach Motta failed me when I should have received the "C" grade I earned, knowing deep down he falsified documents and failed a young kid over a personal issue. Did he even think twice about it? *Probably not.* Think about it for a moment. I was a kid, and a grown man failed me because of his hate for me. I didn't graduate because I was short a few credits.

I should mention too that the entire class of 1982

was special. Our wrestling team took first place in the state, and our track team took third. We had great talent in basketball, most notably in football, but we didn't have the right leadership on the varsity level.

To this day, there has never been a black head coach at the varsity level for basketball, nor has there been one for football at Bloom Trail High School. Even though this is a terrible and quiet injustice to generations of young black teens coming out of poor communities, it was simultaneously an injustice to black men like Ernie Turner, an outstanding and excellent coach. He was clearly qualified for the job. He had the experience and the most time in of all the coaches at the school.

The football players, both white and black, signed a written petition for Coach Turner. Still, the administration didn't give him the job. Therefore, we, as players, were dealing with a form of racism on the football field. The adult black man, Ernie Turner, was also dealing with it on another level.

Racism can be very subtle, but the damages have crushed thousands of blacks in many areas of our lives. One good thing did come out of this when Coach Turner became the assistant principal. I heard he did a spectacular job in his capacity. I am happy for him, but still, I get disgusted when I consider the decades of young black men forced to play their senior year of basketball and football under racist white coaches.

I also made the varsity basketball team. I remember our coach was Pete Maguire, another white man whom I never thought had any experience of playing organized basketball. He struck me as a white man who achieved his educational requirement to coach at the high school level but never played the game himself. To me, he had no clue how to win. I ended up quitting because I didn't want to play for him. His coaching style was not fit for young black men. We were used to running, fast-breaking, and just playing our game to our talents.

We used to reign supreme, traveling around the neighborhoods playing ball. He really put handcuffs on our game. It's like the movie *Hoosiers*. He wanted us to be like that when everybody comes down court and passes to the center in the middle of each play. As far as I was concerned, that was an outdated-ass *white boy* style of playing.

I remember Coach Maguire use to run our tongues out in practice. He got us in great shape. What was stupid to me, was being in excellent condition that prepared us to outlast the other teams because of our endurance. It was a contradiction to his outdated *Hoosier* style of playing the game. The plays were designed to give the ball to the big man every time down the court. I felt like an extremely outstanding point/scoring guard dialing down my game, rushing down the court to set up plays for an average center.

He didn't let us be the racing thoroughbreds we were. After the games, I still had more energy left. If we were winning, then I would have bought into his system, but we were getting our ass kicked. I was a winner, so I began to take matters into my own hands to keep us in the game. He would take me out for deviating against his antiquated playbook, but when we went around on our own and played some of these same guys in the neighborhoods without the coach's involvement, we *would* shoot their asses off the court. *Go figure.*

I remember Coach Maguire brought up a sophomore to start in front of seniors. Not because the sophomore was a better player; frankly speaking, he wasn't, but that was what the coach wanted to do because he liked the kid. That was like throwing my once-in-a-lifetime senior year in the garbage because the coach felt like it.

It might be unfair to label Coach Maguire as a racist. I didn't see much of that in him. He even had a black woman with him at our away games. I never saw him with a black woman around the school or at our home games. I'm not sure what that means, but I will say he wasn't fit to coach a bunch of black kids from East Chicago Heights.

In my opinion, hate is the eighth most deadly sin. I cannot imagine how black men (who never even had a chance to attend school to pursue their dreams) felt. (Think of slavery since the 1500s and the number of blacks who died a slave.) There should be an educational class on *What Hate Looks Like* and how to deal with it. Preparing youngsters for this type of learning would improve the landscape of self-esteem and ego. To my knowledge, there is no formal teaching on this subject matter. It is a massive part of the everyday lives of many youths. How is a child without love supposed to process such actions?

Hate really threw me off. You see, for an exceptionally long time, I thought I deserved what was being thrown at me. There was no one in my home to offset it with positive reinforcement of love and confidence. However, through the years, I've learned, most of the time, it was just the way people dealt with their own insecurities. They really don't hate you. What they hate is "the something" about you that reminds them of an aspect of themselves they wish was better.

Branded

There were some tears and sad times in my life as a teen. I remember surviving the death of my mother, who passed one week before my 14th birthday. I remember taking the call from the doctor when he said, "I'm sorry to break the news to you." I remember bracing. He then said, "Your mother has passed away." I remember this tragic moment vividly.

I can recall the pain I felt as I write about this sad time in my life, 42 years later. It felt like someone had taken a knife and cut an organ out from my body. The cut created a hole inside me that still leaks moments of sadness. Some say it will never completely heal; I'm inclined to agree. That experience was devastating, but you adjust to living with it. It is like living with a hole inside you. There is no one like a mother. Mama is the lifeline that brought us into existence. When that lifeline is no longer present, it's like a little young cub losing its salvation.

My mother was a single parent all my life. She worked two jobs to support four children. My time as a child was spent mostly with my sister, who watched over me as my mother worked. My sister was 10 years older than me, and by the time I was 10, she had given birth to her first child.

My mother had a stroke on the job. I remember seeing her in the hospital on a breathing machine. A few days later, she passed on. I never knew her as well as I would have liked to. It seemed like supporting us all by herself was heavily burdening to her; she used to come home very exhausted. I remember seeing her taking sleeping pills just to get ready for the next day.

I believe my mother worked herself to death. Our time together was minimal; I was a teenager. I came to realize millions of youngsters have similar experiences, and millions more have worse ones. I've seen starving children. It taught me to be thankful for the life I had.

I feel the lessons life has given me took away part of my childhood that remains vacant with me today. It's as though I saw just a little too much, too soon. I was still an adolescent when I experienced some devastating tragedies, and I wasn't developed enough to handle them. Then again, is anyone ever ready for what life brings? To a small degree, those experiences made me a misfit to my peer group. I became too old before my time. I was "old too soon; smart too late."

Two years after my mother passed, my grandfather died. I was devastated emotionally in parts of my early life. Although my grandfather lived in Kentucky, he was the only man ever to call me

"Son." He made me feel the love a son should feel from his father. I never felt this from my birth father, who babysat me a few weeks in a few summers during my adolescent years.

I hadn't healed from the loss of my mother when my grandfather passed. To lose them both in such a short window of time was crushing. I felt there was no one responsible for me anymore. To have these feelings at that age was tough. I felt abandoned, but little did I know this was just a precursor to the emotional devastation I would encounter as a child and an adolescent. The ultimate emotional trauma was yet to come. I was healing a little bit and moving on with my life, but a huge bomb was coming I did not foresee.

One November night in 1982, I remember my childhood homie and I were just hanging out in East Chicago Heights, Illinois. It was the summer following my graduation year. I had fallen a few credit shorts from graduating, and I wanted so badly to enter college. I would have hooped had I got in.

My friends and I went up to the store to get some beer, and my entire life took a hard-left turn. A white woman pulled into the store parking lot. (That rarely happened in my neighborhood.) A single white woman, showing up late at night to kick it with some brothers, was a rarity. After a little conversation, we got in the car with her. My childhood homie couldn't get in because another guy jumped in and beat him to the punch, and the girl said three guys were too many. That was pivotal because the guy who jumped in the front seat turned a simple night of partying with a white girl into a night that changed my life forever.

For me, the time I spent with them was short, maybe 25 minutes max. We drove around for a while, looking for some weed. We were very flirtatious, and she performed oral sex on me briefly. The guy who jumped into the car gradually became a little too aggressive, nothing forceful or violent, just frantic like he had never been with a woman before. I didn't like the tone he was taking, so I left the two of them together. I went back up to the store looking for my homie, but I didn't see him, so I went home.

The next day, my homie told me the girl had gone to the police station and pressed charges on the guy who jumped into the car. He said the police had picked the other guy up and was looking for me. After a little thought, I reacted too quickly. I went to the police station to see Officer Nance because he had seen us sitting in the parking lot together the night before. I came to learn the police weren't looking for me, and had I not gone to the police station, they would have never come looking for me.

The white lady reported the other guy beat her up and raped her the night before. The police found and arrested him. She was said to be on her way back to identify him. I explained to Officer Nance what had happened during the time I was there. He told me she never mentioned me. She only said the guy whom they picked up, and the police were not looking for me.

My homie, Dirty Red, was stupid for telling me the police were looking for me. He is the kind of guy who always runs his mouth without thinking twice about what he says. He thinks to have something to say keeps him relevant but doesn't understand frivolous speaking in many ways is worthless. Still today, he talks without thinking things through. He is one of those guys who needs attention, so he just tells too much to stay in the center of the moment.

I guess because I did nothing to her that would warrant pressing charges, the lady never mentioned another person. Officer Nance called the state's attorney, obviously, and the rest is history. In retrospect, he should have released me because there were no charges against me. Unfortunately, I never left the police station. A few days later, I got indicted. I landed in Cook County Jail, facing charges of kidnapping, rape, and deviate sexual assault. Can you say *nightmare*? I guess officer Nance got his good nigger sticker for calling the state attorney.

During the trial, the victim frequently stated I was a gentleman and genuinely kind to her throughout the time I was present with her. Strangely, somehow, during this gentleman-like and kind behavior of mine, she also said (to my detriment), I *made her* give me oral sex. That was untrue. I couldn't believe she lied. To sum it up, it came out in court like this:

"On November 24, 1982, two teenage boys jumped into the car of a white woman and then forced her to drive somewhere and raped her." I remember the three of us sitting in the parking lot of Shannon's, a liquor store in East Chicago Heights (now Ford Heights). We were parked illegally. Officer Nance pulled up right beside us. He told us to move on, and we couldn't park there.

Officer Nance clearly saw all of us sitting there talking. He knew me because I had lived right across the street from him on Diplomat Lane. He was the stepfather to three of my best childhood friends: Clifford, Reggie, and Stanley Cooper. Clifford and I were like two peas in a pod. Officer Nance never came to testify to what he saw.

You see, what he saw disproves the entire description of what the state's attorneys engineered and presented to the courts. In fact, for some reason, another policeman, Officer Gill, took over the case. Officer Nance was no longer on it; he was an eyewitness and the original arresting officer, but he never was called in to testify in the case.

It turns out going to Officer Nance was one of the biggest mistakes I've ever made in my life. I knew he had seen us sitting in the parking lot. I had done nothing wrong. In my innocence, I wasn't afraid, nor was I unwilling to speak with the police. Well, this decision cost me six years of my life in prison.

Following a jury trial in which 95% of the jury was white, I received a 12-year sentence. The other guy got 18 years. In retrospect, I should have demanded separate trials. At the time, I just didn't understand.

I now have a permanent felony criminal record, a lifelong label that only matters when I meet new people whom I need or want to get close to for some reason. A few years back, a job released me because of a failed criminal background check. That happened in 2014. In truth, I was sentenced to life for that one event at 18 years old.

Thankfully, God was on my side. I never had any major problems in the prison system. Ironically, I was popular inside. I boxed and played basketball. I was instrumental in taking three separate prison basketball teams to the state finals. One of the years, we placed second. Also, I placed second in the Springfield, Illinois Golden Gloves in 1985, while incarcerated. They allowed the prison boxing team to fight in the city's Golden Gloves that year.

Despite being knocked down twice by a three-time Golden Gloves champ, I thought I still won the fight, so did many in the audience who heavily booed as the decision made was in favor of the other guy.

Everybody incarcerated loved sports. I was part of the great entertainment for prisoners. I remember canceling a scheduled fight because I was not feeling well. The next day, the other inmates gave me all kinds of flack because they wanted to see me fight. I also remember one older guy telling me seeing me fight was the only reason he came out to watch the prison boxing matches. That was when the popularity thing really settled in.

Nevertheless, I had literally graduated from a small-time petty stealing youngster to a major league Class X convict in what seemed to be an overnight experience. I tell you this transition is still vivid in my brain today. I've ventured in my mind about the distinction of life on Earth and hell. I use this experience as a sample of what that might be like.

It is a slow death; it killed my spirit. I remember seeing Morgan Freeman in the movie *Shawshank Redemption*. Remember the scene where he was released from prison and went to work for a grocery store? Remember how submissive he was when he kept asking if he could use the restroom, and the manager kept saying to him, "You don't have to ask." I could relate to that character. The prison experience can really break you; it broke me.

It's strange how *it becomes easier for you to live in prison than it does for you to live in the world*. After your spirit is broken, it's like you become institutionalized. When I got out of prison, I was afraid. It's weird how being institutionalized works. I was scared of the world, but I could live in prison comfortably. Isn't that something strange?   In retrospect, I can see how my old homies reacted to me. I mean, I was shaken. I'm sure it came off to them as me being weird or something like that.

Emerging back into society was strange, too. Crack had swept through and changed the world. Most of my old homies were different; I couldn't recognize it at the time, but looking back, I see things better. Crack had recolored people's souls from love to hate literally. After being released from the Mecca of hate, I was starving to find that same ole love from my old homies again, but it was gone. People just weren't the same. Crack had ripped a new hole in the ass of the people in my old neighborhood. It seemed the people, many of my associates and friends, had become dark inside their souls. The wholesomeness and goodness I had once shared were no longer there. Although the world has been full of sin and evil for an awfully long time, crack seemed to have done more damage from the inside out than anything I've ever seen or imagined.

For the most part, I've managed to put that prison episode behind me. I get a little frustrated still when I am rejected from employment because of a background check. Although I don't think I carry a hint or notion of prison on me behind that experience, one thing still cuts at me sometimes. I can still see a clear picture of tears rolling down the white lady's face when the judge sentenced me. I remember looking at her with an expression on my face of *how could you do this me*. As she looked back at me with sorrow on her face, from her left eye, a few tears began falling, and I sensed her saying, "I'm sorry."

Another story worth telling here is about four black guys convicted of raping and murdering two white people when I was a teenager. These four guys lived in my neighborhood. I remember them clearly; they were a little older than I was, but they seemed to be regular guys around the neighborhood. Within a few days, they were gone. They were sentenced to life in prison and ended up spending the next 20 years locked up. The only reason they were released is some Northwestern University students were doing a study. They discovered the DNA found on the two white people did not match the DNA of the four black guys doing time for the crime. Twenty years later, they were released. Many local and national news stations covered this story. I saw them on the news getting released. Imagine if these students had never dug into this story; these men would have spent the rest of their lives in prison for nothing.

What is interesting is while these guys were away from the neighborhood, it somehow became accepted that they must have committed the crime. It's like since they were locked up, they must have been guilty. It's just the way it goes. Then gradually, they are forgotten. *Perception is reality*. Their prison sentences somehow validated their incarceration.

I share some of these experiences only to provide the canvas for this story. There is a parallel between my very own personal tragedy and those suffered by many black men in general. The *artificial reality* we live in is the matrix. I should also add here, unequivocally, that many black men are in prisons because of crimes they committed. Arguably, there are way too many black men incarcerated (in my opinion) who did not deserve to be.

I would say 15% to 20% of black men in prison do not deserve to be there. This problem is real. Imagine if it is easy for white police officers to kill black men in the streets, and get away with it, how easy it is to throw black men into a cage. We have seen police officers beating Rodney King in California and choking the brother to death in New York on video, getting off scot-free. What about gunning down kids with toy guns, shooting a black guy 16 times in the streets, or shooting a black man in the back as he was running away? Remember the killing of a black man in the car with his kid and woman present, or simply choking a guy out for nearly 10 minutes? Well, imagine how easy it is to lock black men up wrongfully, with impunity, back when there were no camera phones or social media. These incidents don't even make the news. It just happens bogusly. It's been going on for centuries.

White Supreminati, I hate you for what you have done to my people and me. You are devils. You will meet God someday, and I hope it's in the flesh.

I remember riding to California with a friend one day. The police *allegedly* stopped him for speeding. I tell you, these police officers wanted to kill us. It was broad daylight, and they got out of the car with their guns drawn, aiming at us with a fierce and deadly look in their eyes. They were screaming at us like we had committed a crime. If I had done anything like scratch my ass or dig in my nose, they would have shot me.

That incident was kind of terrifying, mainly because I felt the energy of the police and knew they wanted to shoot us to release that energy. We were stopped for speeding. There was no criminal suspicion of any sort from us. The vehicle was not stolen; this was simply a traffic stop, and I was staring down the barrel of a gun. I asked the officer, "Why am I fearing for my life here? This is only a traffic stop." He said in a nasty tone, "You're lucky you're not going to jail."

There are so many brothers locked up unjustly, organizations have been formed to address false imprisonment in the U.S. like:

- www.InnocenceProject.org.
- www.AidWYC.org.
- www.ReformingJustice.com.

I imagine if a traumatized person or group is not treated or helped, they will function in abnormality. I have, at times. Many young blacks today are in a horrendous situation, specifically the black family and community as a whole.

Have you ever seen a very traumatized dog or a badly battered man or woman? White supremacists broke the spirit of the black race here in the U.S. in the same manner. They disconnected blacks from their culture, their religion, their land, and their family. They slaughtered, murdered, and hung our little boys. Many males had their penises cut off to stop reproduction. These traumatic experiences were committed against blacks for centuries, and no one apologized nor even attempted to repair it.

I consider of all the trouble Michael Vick got into for dog-fighting. I remember when I was a teenager and the older boys in my neighborhood used to do the same thing with Pit Bulls. That was about 38 years ago or more. Imagine all the dead/traumatized dogs that have suffered from this throughout the world. But tell me, isn't this treatment of dogs very much like the same thing whites did to black people? Torture, kill, and pit blacks against each other? Pit Bulls. Pit Blacks.

What whites did to black people was far worse. As an animal lover, I'm glad there was a healing process for the surviving dogs involved in that scandal. It's a shame blacks have never received a healing process from America. Blacks are still getting gunned down. Have you heard of any type of program by whites called *Healing the Black Community?* Was the treatment of blacks in this country not worthy of healing?

Whites speak down on black ghettos today, talking about how bad and disgusting they are, yet treat battered dysfunctional dogs after their horrific experience from fighting and exploitation. Following the horrible experience of being black in America, you jail us, shoot us, and discriminate against us as if our dysfunction is worth less than that of Pit Bulls. You have treated black people worse than dogs *literally*. Still today, America has shown more remorse for those dogs than they have shown for black people. While justified in giving the Eskimos and the Indians reparations, this country has put up the middle finger to blacks. Why isn't there any collective remorse for what they have done to the black community?

Imagine if the general society of whites hated those dogs like blacks have been hated since slavery. If we kicked those dogs and threw bricks at them all the time, what would the dogs be like? They would be considered dysfunctional and dangerous to society at large. Although blacks are not chained up anymore, the oppression from whites has been poured heftily on blacks. We are gunned down by police officers, bitten by dogs, beaten with clubs, sprayed with water hoses, called out of our names, imprisoned disproportionately, discriminated from jobs—all *post*-slavery. Doesn't this mean whites still hate backs?

All that has happened occurred just to have the right to an adequate education, the right to vote, or of course, the necessity for affirmative action (once described by former Ambassador Alan Keyes as "affirmative apartheid").

Whites are quick to blow it off as something that happened years ago, but like the dogs in the Michael Vick case or anything that is traumatized, if there is no healing process, then it will live on with dysfunctional behavior. This is how social engineering works. This is the mission of The Supreminati. It is exactly the behavior they have designed to denigrate black people. It is why they have no remorse; they are not sorry for their actions. The strategy was and is a success to them. It is a *fete accompli*. Therefore the black man and woman cannot link together strongly for their family and their community.

Boom

(What Your People Really Did to Blacks)

During the Willie Lynch era, a virus was inserted deliberately into black people. It was not a biological virus. It was psychological; it is much more lethal. Today's whites are not the founding culprits for this cunning ploy against black men and women; however, this virus was inserted centuries ago, *way* before their time. Nevertheless, an effort has sustained and kept this ploy alive since the days of slavery. That means the implementation of the scheme, although initiated in the 1600s, has been carried on through to 2020. The baton has passed on through centuries. We know Willie Lynch taught this ploy to slave masters.

Since there are no more slave masters (technically), then to whom was the baton passed to? Of course, no one would ever take ownership of being the replacement of slave owners, so The Supreminati became more sophisticated with their strategy.

When I first read about Willie Lynch, I could not believe any human created by God could do such horrible things to another human being. The acts committed reminds me of life in the wild, the jungle. Think about how lions and hyenas rip apart a newborn baby buffalo or a baby zebra. For the animals, these acts are for survival. It's the way of the jungle for wild animals. In the case of whites doing the same to black people, these acts were committed to reprogram black people into a dysfunctional behavior that would ensure a self-inflicted state of destruction lasting hundreds or thousands of years.

Willie Lynch was a slave owner who invited other slave owners to a seminar (so to speak). He taught them how to train their slaves to be willing participants in their own life-long self-destruction. Below is an excerpt taken directly from the Willie Lynch letters:

*"Take the meanest and most restless nigger, strip him of his clothes in front of the remaining male niggers, the female, and the nigger infant, tar and feather him, tie each leg to a different horse faced in opposite directions, set him afire and beat both horses to pull him apart in front of the remaining niggers. The next step is to take a bullwhip and beat the remaining nigger males to the point of death, in front of the female and the infant. Don't kill him but **put the fear of God in him** so he can be useful for future breeding.* (2009, FinancialCall.com News)

To dismantle human beings and rip them apart in front of their families for subconscious reprogramming and economic gain is beyond the behavior of wild animals. I am not being fair to wild animals when I compare them to this manner of

American slave owners. Can you imagine a deer's fear of a pack of lions? Blacks were being traumatized. Imagine what young children and women felt as they witnessed these acts. How could these slave-owning white people be so damned cruel?

When I finally settled down to put things into perspective, it was clear that a doctrine was taught to white people. It makes me think of a trade school, or a training course you take to be a mechanic, or how to become an accountant or computer programmer, electrician, or any type of skilled laborer. In this case, white people were taught the trade of how to keep the black community functioning in a way that would keep them in a self-destructive mode for hundreds or maybe thousands of years.

The Willie Lynch teaching ensured long-lasting disunity among black people. I remember reading about this ploy. It was designed to take fear, envy, and distrust and make these emotions bigger. Another way of looking at it is to put each of these emotions on steroids, and they would be so huge they would have permanent side effects. When I look at the behavior of black people today and tie it to the design of this evil ploy, the script for blacks (many years ago) is like a movie script today. Only this script was designed for the stage of life. Where it differs from a movie script is that it was inserted inconspicuously and cunningly into black behavior. Basically, it is a stealth script for black people.

The WLMF (Willie Lynch Mind Fuck) is the cunning evil force that's changed the course of building the family for black people. While successful in destroying the development of generations of black men, the additional collateral damage is that it forced the black woman into a *superwoman-like* behavior. She had to carry the family (i.e. community) on her shoulders.

If the WLMF was building up the black man, it

would have strengthened the black culture, but it didn't. It tore down the black man. That created an imbalance in the black family structure; it was the primary objective of the WLMF. The way to kill off an ethnicity of people is to take away their ability to reproduce themselves. This mind-fuck has weakened our reproduction enormously. Instead of the black population being at only 40 million in the US, the number should probably be over 140 million.

Not only has the WLMF pitted the black man and woman against each other, but it has also created many other divisions between black men. We are at war with each other in our neighborhoods over issues like gangs, colors, complexions, and class differences. *It is a life of hating the next person because of what they've got.* Here is another piece taken directly from the Willie Lynch letters (all emphasis added):

I HAVE A FOOL-PROOF METHOD FOR

CONTROLLING YOUR BLACK SLAVES. I guarantee every one of you that, if installed correctly, IT WILL CONTROL THE SLAVES FOR AT LEAST 300 HUNDRED YEARS. My method is simple. Any member of your family or your overseer can use it. I HAVE OUTLINED A NUMBER OF DIFFERENCES AMONG THE SLAVES, AND I TAKE THESE DIFFERENCES AND MAKE THEM BIGGER. I USE FEAR, DISTRUST, AND ENVY FOR CONTROL PURPOSES. These methods have worked on my modest plantation in the West Indies, and it will work throughout the South. Take this simple little list of differences and think about them. On top of my list is "AGE," but it's there only because it starts with an "a." The second is "COLOR" or shade. There is INTELLIGENCE, SIZE, SEX, SIZES OF PLANTATIONS, STATUS on plantations, ATTITUDE of owners, whether the slaves live in the valley, on a hill, East, West, North, South, have fine hair, coarse hair, or is tall or short. Now that you have a list of differences, I shall give you an outline of action, but before that, I shall assure you that DISTRUST IS STRONGER THAN TRUST AND ENVY STRONGER THAN ADULATION, RESPECT OR ADMIRATION. The black slaves, after receiving this indoctrination shall carry on and will become self-refueling and self-generating for HUNDREDS of years, maybe THOUSANDS. Don't forget; you must pitch the OLD black male vs. the YOUNG black male and the YOUNG black male against the OLD black male. You must use the DARK skin slaves vs. the LIGHT skin slaves, and the LIGHT skin slaves vs. the DARK skin slaves. You must use the FEMALE vs. the MALE, and the MALE vs. the FEMALE. You must also have white servants and overseers [who] distrust all blacks. But it is NECESSARY THAT YOUR SLAVES TRUST AND DEPEND ON US. THEY MUST LOVE, RESPECT, AND TRUST ONLY US. Gentlemen, these kits are your keys to control. Use them. Have your wives and children use them, never miss an opportunity. IF USED

INTENSELY FOR ONE YEAR, THE SLAVES THEMSELVES WILL REMAIN PERPETUALLY DISTRUSTFUL. Thank you, gentlemen. (2009, Financial.com News)

The war within our very own people is the very reason why we are not fruitful and freely multiplying. That is the exact opposite of the intended purpose given to us by God for life. What an evil thing to do to a group of people. I do believe there is a devil that works through the human flesh. In this instance, he came through white supremacists.

Let us look at the black woman. The core most significant detriment resulting from the WLMF was to divide the black woman away from her king: the black man. They represent the head and our people, the body. Kill the head, and the body will follow. They damaged our heads by dividing and conquering the soul and mind of the black man and woman. Now, the body is falling.

The black children, along with the entire black family, find themselves in horrible situations. Biblically speaking, the man is the head of the family. The black man was torn apart by being tied to two horses facing opposite directions and then pulled until he was physically split in half and destroyed. Black families were forced to witness these cruel and traumatic horrors inflicted upon the one whom they viewed as their leader, protector, provider, and king: the black man.

Think about this for a moment: imagine what times were like back then. Unlike the more progressed attitude of blacks today, during slavery, white men with guns brought blacks to this strange country. These white men murdered, raped, lynched, and slaughtered blacks for just being what they coined a 'nigger.'

If you saw your father, uncle, big brother, and male cousins begging for their life, as they were being slaughtered in the middle of your block, how would you feel? In a way that cows are slaughtered to be packaged and put in a grocery store, how would you feel? Can you imagine the fear and terror black women and children felt as they witnessed this? I cannot. It is too much for me to stomach, but maybe through these acts, they were convinced their black king or family leader wasn't so strong after all. Blacks had no guns during this perilous time and could not defend themselves or their families. They only had a fear of white slave owners. Ironically, that fear was probably greater than the fear of God. That was *absolute trauma*.

Think of the Rodney King beating that occurred on the streets of California—at the hands of police officers. Was that a modern-day version of white hate on black men? As long ago as the Rodney King beating was, or as current as George Floyd or Black Lives Matter, do you think healing for blacks is a real possibility with white police officers still behaving this way? Did you see those white men brutally beating that helpless black man almost 20 years ago or choking the other nearly 20 years later? Hate was equally pouring out of those police officers. The hate was out of control. Years ago, Rodney died by drowning. I am convinced that beating probably contributed to his early death.

Reflect one moment and view the number of police officers beating this handcuffed man lying on the ground. They were beating this man as though he killed their mother. Tell me what was really coming out from these white men. Was it something natural, or was it something else? That clearly isn't the motto of America's police of "To Protect and to Serve."

Now think about 2014 when a Chicago kid got shot 16 times by an officer for nothing. The kid was just walking and got shot—16 times! Tell me what was coming out from this officer. With that being possible, how easy is it to just imprison a black man? That's why the jails are full of black men.

Even more recently with the murder of George Floyd, can you imagine the number of similar incidents never caught on tape that have not been exposed to the public-at-large? Social media now brings it all to us. Try and imagine when the police did not have social media to worry about—no camera phones nor a place to post it for the world to see. There are an untold number of incidents we will never know about—the countless victims living life as the walking wounded.

All the rights blacks have in this country were fought for, as well as died for. White people did not wake up and voluntarily say, "Let's allow blacks to go to school, or vote, or give them affirmative action," or anything for that matter. That means hate and the subscription to supremacist beliefs didn't flee voluntarily from them. They didn't decide to be fair on their own; blacks had to march, picket, die, and sacrifice their lives for *some* justice. Therefore, the hate didn't just leave; it just compromised with black people, which means it is still there.

To think the U.S. government funded reparations for Native Americans and Eskimos but have no funding worthy of giving to black people speaks volumes about this country's true feelings towards blacks. To this day, black people are still being gunned down in the streets by white law enforcement men. I guess the black officers do not encounter the same type of threats from young black men as white officers.

We are still fighting racism today. Despite the consistent effort of many white people to downplay racism and question blacks' interpretation of every event that has the race element in it, black people know (for a fact) it still exists in the everyday lives of blacks. *To think* this government doesn't see the 400 years of slavery worthy enough to give reparations to blacks makes a clear statement to me.

I don't expect ever to see America give reparation to black people, but I do want to make the point that while the Indians enjoy their casinos and the Eskimos have their land, many black people will wake up tomorrow and deal with some form of racism—a Travon Martin or a Michael Brown type of incident. Whites will continue to deny this fact that blacks are still dealing with it daily, combined with the fact that the government and/or The Supreminati have never shown acts of remorse. That shows me the powers are against black people permanently and have invisibly put their middle finger up to us.

When I envision those white police officers beating Rodney King or even today choking Eric Gardner or George Floyd, their hostile actions said, "We had to deal with you niggers, but still, this is what we really feel." This sums up what blacks can expect from America.

Role Reversal

(Perhaps the Worst Crime of All)

Killing the head is a process, not just a one-time act. When I consider the many civil rights fights and the job opportunities denied to black men, I am convinced it is a continuation in the process of killing the head. Man is supposed to be the leader and provider of his household. Without adequate education and employment, he is unable to fulfill his role in leading a family. In turn, he is then disqualified from passing ethical values to the next generation. He then turns to alternatives, which, in most cases, are criminal actions and behaviors. Potentially drugs, alcohol, and other addictions come into play. Before you know it, prison becomes part of his life.

Understandably, the black woman loses respect for

him. She is then left alone without a man, and her view of her fallen black king becomes hopeless. She is forced to make ends meet for herself and her children. Did any other ethnicity of women have to experience this? This very point is where the black family began a downward spiral. The black woman has said, "Fuck the black man. I don't need no man to take care of myself." In the act of self-preservation, she has rebelled and defected the black man, not even considering an evil force was behind it all.

The black family was partially salvaged and rescued. The black woman held up what was left, but the flip-side of this was the black family (as a unit) broke apart. That was by design/social engineering. It is precisely the break the social engineers intended. Ironically, without her taking this stand, the black community would not have a chance to rebound today; therefore, the black woman kept our people alive.

Government-funded White Supremacy has rewarded the black woman with an aid check to keep the black man out of the home. I've heard some say she is, perhaps, the strongest living species. In the proper perspective, I now believe this: it is mainly due to the white supremacist, ensuring that the black man would never become a strong species, let alone the strongest species. That was the white man's fear, because if black men had flourished, then the white men would be guaranteed a formidable adversary. Therefore, through trickery and social engineering, he destroyed and weakened black men.

Consequently, many black women have celebrated their esteem in America as being considered stronger than the black man. To me, this only furthers The Supreminati's agenda. While black women compete to wear this title proudly (actually, eat it up), I never hear this gender argument about who is the strongest within any other group of people; only black people—another cunning division imposed upon us.

This occurrence represented a critical moment in dividing black people. This process forced black women into complete independence. On the surface, this should not be a bad thing. From a logical standpoint, having two breadwinners should make a unit twice as strong; however, it didn't seem to play out that way. I must also add I cannot recall a time where white, Hispanic, Chinese, Japanese, or women from any other nationalities, carried such a burden. That explains why the family structure of different nationalities is more solidified than within black families.

The black woman took over the driver's seat of the black family, strictly out of necessity. She allowed the black man to ride with her occasionally. Due to the systematic destruction of the black man, he was relegated to the back seat.

Look at white women, Chinese women, Hispanic women, European women, and women from other nationalities. They are not like black women. Black women became hardened because of the residual effects of the WLMF. When I say hardened, I don't mean anything negative. I mean, she had to tap into her male hormones more than any other woman did. The black woman was hardened, and the black man was broken down, reduced, and weakened.

Women from other nationalities don't seem to have the attitude of, "I don't need no man to do shit for me." If you look at women from other nationalities, they are not as out front and in-your-face as black women are. The demeanor of other women is subtle, in the rear, and soft-spoken. They seem extremely comfortable in the role they are in. On the other hand, black women are the opposite. They are more out front—engaged and edgy. Their characteristics are blatant and have much more of a stronger presence that speaks loudly. They had to be this way. The WLMF removed the black man's strength (and presence) from her life, so she compensated.

The black woman was forced to tap more into her testosterone to cope with what life gave her. It's natural. If one of our senses is lost, it forces the other senses to get stronger. The same thing applies here. If nature held a contest to find an Alpha-male within the female gender, black women would win.

I often hear black women talk about black men who date white women: "He can't handle a strong black woman, so he goes for a submissive white woman." Additional statements are: "Black men don't want to do shit," or "Black men are all dogs. They are lazy and perpetually cheat on their women constantly." Although he may go after white women sometimes, the sisters' reasoning may be a little skewed (to me). He is adapting to an action that systematically got instituted to separate him from his own. That is the reaction, not the first action.

In turn, I often hear black men say things like, "Sisters are too hard to deal with," "Sisters are a big battle to deal with," or "They are pissed-off and angry all the time." To me, it seems both are right, and this is what the WLMF was designed to accomplish precisely: to create conflict. It worked; it *really* worked.

I don't think people of other races talk this way about each other. I've heard black men say they don't date black women. I've also heard black women say they don't date black men. Does any other societal group suffer from this? Have you ever listened to a Latino woman saying she doesn't date Latino men, or Asian and white women (in large scale numbers) saying they don't date their own? Perhaps, there are a few isolated cases in all groups of people, but overall, I haven't seen this same type of behavior on a large scale for others as I have from black people.

We see many successful black men with white

women, and many beautiful black women with white men for different reasons. In the black man's case, he has been through hell in this country that the easygoing, light attitude, white women can give him relief from and rest of mind. He has a lot of pressure on him to be in the position he is in. To some degree, he just needs someone to play with to provide a balance to his life. It is like having a puppy; you often hear white women referred to as a "Barbie doll." The white woman can play along with the black man. She doesn't have the baggage of struggle the black woman had to confront or be burdened with. She didn't endure the WLMF, so yes, she can be the little Barbie doll-like puppy to play with. He has been burdened so heavily, someone who keeps it light feels good to him again. The black woman was once light-hearted, but her lightness has been stolen from her.

I believe retribution plays a small part here. Remember, white men impregnated black women intentionally during slavery. I believe the design was to create lighter-skinned blacks as part of the ploy to create divisions within the black race. Perhaps, the black man gets a kick out of returning the act of banging the white man's most precious possession: the white woman.

In the case of the successful black woman who rolls with the white man, this is a case of too few qualified black men. The black woman has become tired of the routine of having a black man not cutting it, especially financially. She, too, wants the finer things in life.

Many successful white men in this country have old money. Even their offspring comes into the world with a family legacy to ride on. For a long time, they have been able to show beautiful black women a life the black men couldn't afford. They could buy diamonds, take them on trips to foreign countries, buy them a house, or set them up in an expensive apartment with the rent paid for months. Brothers, on the other hand, often struggle on their blue-collar jobs just to make ends meet.

When I see white men with black women, most of the time, she is the cream of the black crop. When I see black men with white women, it seems as if only the pro-athlete and movie star black men get the cream of the white crop. In the lower class, black men with white women are… Well, I'm sure you know the rest of that story.

I can tell white men really hate seeing brothers with white women. They may even hate it worse than the sisters hate the reverse scenario. I admit I don't like seeing beautiful black women with white men because I don't believe they earned them. They attracted them because of the life-long benefits they receive simply for living with white favor.

I always wonder if the white man feared the brothers' sperm could color the population black. Whites created divisions in black skin color intentionally by impregnating or breeding, as they called it, through black women. I wonder if black men need to keep screwing white women until we are all the same hue or color? I heard one black man's sperm could color a nation of 25,000 whites.

I believe this is the travesty that has mind-fucked us all as black people. I say again: we are not the way we are with each other by chance. We've been made complete guinea pigs by an evil force. It is a terrible mistake to say this only happened a long time ago. To think of it in that way ignores the fact that it was a long-term strategy. Willie Lynch stated it could last 300 years, maybe even thousands. I personally think he nailed it.

Slavery was a horrible thing, but this shit is much deeper. It is still effective in keeping blacks divided. No other community of men and women are divided the way blacks are. I wish we would work collectively at healing this horrible act that has been placed upon our culture. However, I might be a dreamer in this area of thinking.

My conclusion on this thought is that Willie Lynch reprogramming changed the course of human nature for black people. By destroying the black man in the manner The Supreminati has in America, and continues to do, it has made it unlikely for an average black man to fulfill his role as the head adequately. That reduces the number of qualified black men, which, in turn, forces the black woman to step in and become the head. The plan reversed the roles. The design was to make the black woman submissive to the white man's power instead of the black man, and for a very long time, it was successful; however, at some point, she was fed up and became stronger because of it. It brought out the absolute best in black women. *The destruction of the black men brought out the best in black women.*

The black woman has outdone the black man. She is more educated, and she has more opportunities in America than the black man does. In her mind, she has surpassed the black man. She has become psychologically superior, compared to her black king, and she tends to wear it on her sleeve. It makes an implicit reference to her (imported) elitist belief over the black man. That defines her mindset from the start. It is not good for the union because she probably has made this a standard. If this is true, then it is not in alignment with divine order. That was all done at the hand of Willie Lynch and his ilk, *destroy the union*. In so doing, you curtail reproduction *and* achieve defacto population control. You destroy family-building, which, consequently, has a devastating ripple effect in every aspect of black life. *It's genocide, my friends*.

I must say even this ploy seems to have run its course. It appears for a long time, our sisters flaunted and reveled in their role of outdoing and upstaging brothers. You've heard the song, *Run the World [Girls]* about women ruling by Beyoncé, and the *Black Girls Rock* television program, which has become a serious black women's movement. I absolutely love the mentoring and positive example they (*Black Girls Rock*) provide for young black teens across the nation. Black women held the black community together for a long time. Without them being single parents of many black households, where would we be today? But now, the sisters are experiencing the other side of this out-performance they've demonstrated over the brothers.

While black women are just being strong and "being a sister," the cunning and divisive thing that's happening is propelling them away from many black men. Many are now lonely and are missing a man to complete their lives. Even though they have stability, homes, and good careers, there is the void of an equally-yoked "brother" in their lives.

In my opinion, this primary thing keeps black men and women from becoming the kind of union the black community needs so badly. There is an imbalance. We have the few successful and popular black men, with a buffet of beautiful, successful black women to choose from. He is a treasure to them, like a rare coin. They often chase after him. Many black women lay at his feet, as it were. It becomes difficult for him to be faithful to one black woman, and the moment he chooses to take more than one from the buffet, he is then labeled unfaithful and a dog. Then the perpetual slander of the black man's image continues.

Likewise, there are too few successful black men. Accordingly, the black woman refuses to settle for less. She often brings more to the table than the many black men she is left to choose from; thereby, involving herself with him, a black woman might see this as lowering her standards. She is right—sort of.

It is understandable how the black woman feels a bit twisted. Divine order would always have the man bringing more to the table, and if you look at other groups of people, divine order, for the most part, is intact; however, not with blacks. What is so wrong is how these circumstances came about.

To think a strategy was implemented to create an imbalance between black men and black women is too unbelievable to fathom. Still, I tell you, if you want to prevent a group of people from surpassing 100,000,000, then you damage the area capable of creating it—in this case, the relationship between the black woman and the black man. Again I tell you, it's genocide, and it's clever.

I once read white men run 97% of all Fortune 500 companies. That is also probably true throughout all Fortune 10,000 companies. Let's say you are a white male executive of a Fortune 500 company looking to hire someone of color to fill a position within the organization. Since black women are graduating from college at a much higher rate than black men, let's say there are four black women and one black man vying for the job. Each of the female candidates is black and beautiful, sexy and smart, on the order of Halle Berry or Beyoncé. Now, on the other hand, the one brother applying is sharp as a whip himself—polished and built strong with an upright physical stature of a professional football or basketball player. Who do you think the white man is most likely to hire? Even if there are four black men and one black woman, who do you think will get the job?

Whether a Fortune 500 company or a local family-owned business, this scenario is common from coast to coast. The white man would hire the black woman much more often than the black man. I am not implying that sexism is the compelling reason, but also not suggesting it isn't either.

I honestly believe most white men fear a strong black man. I am not sure if it is just a natural thing or if it is generational guilt of some sort. Still, think about it. If you had a 200-pound Rottweiler that you've beaten and abused for more than 400 years, wouldn't it make sense that you would be a little scared of it?

The black woman has not been as beaten down by The Supreminati as the black man has. The reason is the white man does not fear her. At her best, the white man is secured safely in his dominance. Yet, the black man, at his best, threatens the white man. I am not chauvinistic when I say this; the black man is one thing the white man fears because the black man can overtake him. For the most part, the black woman does not pose the same threat. That is the reason there is an argument about who is the strongest between black men and black women. The Supreminati wanted it that way, and they achieved it.

Slave Trading:
Damn, Y'all Sick

While in prison in my early adulthood, I would see brothers get released, but then return after having freedom for a short while. I often wondered how and why a large percentage of brothers kept coming back to prison. The recidivism rate was disturbing. It seemed like black men were the biggest losers. I told myself I never want to be caught in this revolving cycle. Little did I know my turn would come.

I was released from prison in 1988, and less than four years later, I was back in again. This time, my crime was being a black man wearing a red jacket. A female purse-snatching victim described a black man in a red jacket. I remember sitting in my cell reading the police report on this purse-snatching case that had been put on me.

The thing I remember most about the police report is *five minutes*. According to the report, at 7:15 pm on a weeknight on the north side of Chicago, a white woman informed the police she fought with and sprayed mace in the face of a black man who snatched her purse. I was picked up at 7:20 pm, the same night, about one block away from where the crime took place, which was where I lived at the time.

The police searched me; I was wearing a red jacket that night. I even let them go into my apartment, although I didn't know what they were looking for at the time. Within minutes after being picked up, the police drove me around to the scene of the crime. It took about two minutes to get there. As I sat handcuffed in the backseat of the car, I will never forget how the white police driver jumped out of the vehicle and confidently said, "We got the guy who snatched your purse."

The white lady walked up to the rear driver's side window. She looked inside the car, and there she saw a black man, handcuffed, wearing a red jacket at nighttime. This time, it was me. She said, "Yeah, that's him."

Regardless of it being a five-minute difference between the crime getting committed and the time I was picked up (according to the police report), no one seemed to give a fuck that I had not been sprayed with mace, nor did I have any of her belongings. There was no trace of evidence that I had been in a struggle of any sort.

I remember one of the three police officers in the car as we drove to the station, saying to me, "I don't believe you did it." I asked him, "Why don't you tell her that?" To which he replied, "How am I supposed to tell her that? She thinks it was you."

I pointed out the crime just happened to her, and she

was probably not in the right state of mind. I also mentioned the police driver jumping out and telling her, "We've got the guy who snatched your purse." The lady never really looked at my face. What was she supposed to think?

If you ever heard a black man doesn't stand much of a chance in the criminal court system, then try giving a little thought to what it's like for a black man, with a previous record, reappearing in court. Better yet, just visit him in prison and get all your answers from him directly.

Somehow, I'd become part of this vicious cycle of repeat offenders. Now, I didn't think for one minute most repeat offenders get railroaded in the manner I was; I was just learning a sad lesson. Our so-called justice system wasn't seeking justice. It was merely business-as-usual, going through the motions.

First, they give you a bond they know you can't afford. Then they make you sit in the county *hell-*

cell in 45-day increments, waiting to see a judge. You then go in front of a judge for 15 seconds, and he/she gives you a continuance for another 60 days just to repeat the same process. Nine months later, you are happy to have any semblance of forward motion in your life.

I was taken to prison, where I was totally worn down from the inhumane treatment from nine months of being in the stink at Cook County Jail. Strangely, I was damn-near happy to go to prison. I took a plea-bargain just to get the hell away from the county jail.

Believe it or not, more than 85% of cases go down like that. The strategy is to wear you down in the county jail, then offer you a small plea. Meanwhile, some thief in a red jacket is living scot-free and plotting to steal another woman's property the first chance he gets. It is only the conviction they want..

I was released after 18 months. By that time, I had

to start my life over again from scratch. When I got arrested, my girlfriend was in Minnesota, auditioning to become a dancer. It was such a shock to her when she had to come back because I had gotten locked up. This ordeal ruined our relationship, and she moved on with her life. The burden of being with a man in prison was probably too much for her.

Going through that was very painful; she was a wonderful girl, and I loved her. Although I did get to see her once after I was released, we never got back together. She was 22 years of age at the time, and it's understandable how she must've felt. I did "see" her in the Ice Cube movie, *Barbershop*. I was happy she was working on her dream to be in show business. Still today, she probably never believed I was telling the truth about not having anything to do with the crime.

The funny thing is most people don't believe you can go to prison falsely. People just don't think it when you tell them you had absolutely nothing to do with a crime. I remember my own sister asking with a peculiar tone, "What *really* happened?"

I am amazed at how much trust the average person has that our justice system is genuinely good at meting-out justice; it is so fucking corrupt. It's simply big business, especially for black men. Did you know prisons are now on the stock market? You can buy stock in the penal institutions. I'm not happy to tell you this, but if you want a stock tip, prisons are a sure bet. Have you ever heard the term slave-trading? It's legal again. Imagine the speculators in this game.

I remember ABC's Ted Kopple did a series on overcrowding in the prison population some years ago. He reported that prisons are bursting at the seams. It appears to me, the government and its justice system in the U.S. are profiting. They seem to treat prison and human life with the same underlying objective as Wal-Mart and McDonald's in their industries. The building of prison prototypes seems to replicate the same franchising model these businesses use to cookie-cut thousands of locations across the nation.

I'm a true believer this happens because of the two separate occasions I went to prison for crimes I did not commit. Charge one, I was present but did not commit the crime I was convicted of. Charge two, I was nowhere around the crime scene, but fit the description of a black man wearing a red jacket. The previous "X" on my back is what sealed the deal, not the purse. It was like a dose of how it felt to be a hopeless slave.

Building a prison stimulates the economy of small rural towns throughout the U.S. We call them "hick towns." Residents of these hick towns can now apply for jobs that didn't exist previously. First, there are construction jobs to build the prison. Next, before you know it, banks, grocery stores, restaurants, retail shops, new schools, and many other commercial services appear. *Voila!* An entire community is developed—around a slave camp. I mean prison, more dollars for the government to tax. It really is organized or legalized slavery.

I'm not implying some people who commit crimes do not deserve a prison sentence. People who commit murder, rape, child molestation, robbery, and home invasion are deserving of prison time. I am merely stating the institution of our justice system is very corrupt. It is White Supremacy at its finest. Cleverly and socially, The Supreminati have manufactured a scheme to enslave blacks legally. Instead of addressing the problems of poverty proactively, by creating real opportunities for young blacks and Hispanics in the hood, they'd rather not because there's money in building prisons. Big money!

Each time a state sentences a person to prison, the federal government sends the state the $30,000, then calculate it for each year. Simply put: the families behind the Federal Reserve go into their money-printing factory and print the money to house a prisoner for a year. It is probably much more than that. I'm sure most states get additional funding while the living conditions of prisoners are reduced tremendously. I could then distinguish what slavery was like. As a prisoner, I was tantamount to a piece of state property. I was no longer a human being; it was just a big business. I never stood a chance. *Imagine that.*

I consider the crooked judges, state attorneys, city/county prosecutors, politicians, and police officers. They feed this cash cow continuously, knowing it is unjust, and they are part of a corrupted society and justice system. I cannot forgive this. You see, these people are holding positions of trust in our society that designed to keep order in our communities and lives. This very institution is corrupt.

Unfortunately, the police officers may get more of

the blame from us since they are on the front line of this corruption. The systemic aspect of this corruption should not be overlooked. The state attorneys and the judges seem to flood this system without getting their hands dirty. I tell you (inside the court system) they cleverly create slave camps. Therefore, it is not possible to have a good community under a corrupt system.

Have you ever been railroaded into prison by this system? Let's do some math here. Today, there are more than two million people incarcerated in the U.S. Two million multiplied by $30,000 equals $60 billion.

Let's look at the numbers a little closer. Black people make up 13% of the U.S. population, roughly around 50,000,000 people overall. Black women, children, and underage teens probably make up the lion's share of the 50,000,000. Leaving how many black men? The answer is perhaps less than 10 to 12,000,000.

Black men make up close to 50% of the U.S. prison population. If the prison population is 2,000,000, that means blacks make up close to 1,000,000. Therefore, the proportionate amount (50 %) of $60 billion is $30 billion to house and incarcerate black men. Again, blacks are only 13% of the population. Adult black men are certainly less than that. The count is maybe 10,000,000 of the 50,000,000. Essentially, adult black men make up what? Maybe 5-6 % of the U.S. male population? Well, *nearly half* of the government spending on prisons goes to incarcerating black men. (5% of the U.S. male population.) Keep in mind my numbers are close estimates. I am trying to paint a picture rather than get the numbers correct. Therefore, if you are doing the math here, then you've already missed the point.

This may be a mere coincidence, or it may not be. Still, it's a form of slavery. On top of this, it creates thousands of jobs throughout the nation (majorly for white people). More white jobs equal more tax revenue. If you translate, it means once you get convicted of a crime, then slavery is permitted. So, it's legal after the courts railroad you into prison.

Understanding now, I see the 13th Amendment, which permits slavery after the conviction of a crime, and I swear to you, I feel like I was *shipped to prison*. Maybe like how the slaves felt when they were shipped to America. Of course, I wasn't in danger of starvation, disease, and laying in my own excrement like my ancestors were to America or the West Indies, but shipped, nonetheless.

My experiences in the court systems were never about the search for the truth. They were mere formalities to satisfy the rights we have as citizens "due process" awarded to us by the Constitution. The entire court process is like a magic trick. The courts, like a magician, can execute this appearance of due process daily, giving the appearance that truth and justice are being searched for and meted out. The truth of the matter is blacks don't stand a "snowball's chance" in the court systems. Nine times out of 10, when a black man goes in front of the criminal court system, he will most likely be convicted and go to prison. It's like a sleight-of-hand trick. (By the way, most judges are white or female).

I saw the *illusion* of due process, but I never saw a real search for truth and justice. I got handled like cattle, so were thousands before me and after. The act of due process was just a mere formality to move me through the system. *Okay, check the box; he got his trial or plea deal.*

The question that comes to mind is: is it a coincidence that the 13th Amendment enables slavery after the punishment of crime and black men (who are slave descendants) make up nearly half the U.S. prison population? America imprisons more people than any other country. Half of that population comes from the people who were once slaves or are still slaves. This trickery makes slavery legal.

That is social engineering at its best. It looks just like slavery, doesn't it? That's the trick. Private citizens cannot have slaves, but the government can—for maybe $.50 a day, working in a prison laundry room or kitchen. I guess it's not real slavery, huh? They do get paid.

Interestingly, all things will run its course. In this case, even this evil ploy to incarcerate black men has been affected by our country going bankrupt. (The printing of dollars by the Feds caught up with them during this past recession.) Our government had to change the laws and free some prisoners because the greed and wickedness of this government came full-circle and bit them in the ass.

I suppose the ploy that undermines the black man is ongoing. I am caught in between whether it is just an *automatic* action or still by design. Black destructionists have sustained this ploy for centuries. What I don't know is if there is a destruction committee of old white men who meet regularly to strategize on keeping the scheme updated and relevant, or if this virus is so cunningly sown into black people's behavioral patterns, psyche, and subconscious. Is it both, or is it just on automatic pilot and impossible to pinpoint?

People say the "slavery stuff" happened centuries ago, so everyone should get past it. That means they do not believe this is an on-going ploy. If that's so, then the culprit has vanished. They cannot realize this is not a conscious effort by black people to fail. Since they do not believe there are black destructionists and/or White Supreminati working to keep blacks down, they have no one else to blame but the black man. They say he's lazy; he always wants a handout, etc.

Isn't it funny the very reason black men were brought to this strange land from their native countries is they were great at working with their hands? Blacks built this country—literally. Yet, today, many of them are labeled lazy, good for nothing, *niggers*. Isn't this ironic?

That is scary. Do any of you remember the movie *Manchurian Candidate* with Denzel Washington playing the lead role? It was about reprogramming people with chemicals. Well, did you consider that Willie Lynch was about reprogramming people through behavioral practice and psychological conditioning? His claim that *"by killing the protective male image, and by creating a submissive dependent mind of the nigger male slave, we have created an orbiting cycle that turns on its own axis forever, unless a phenomenon occurs and re-shifts the position of the male and female slaves."* He nailed it.

The point is clear that America has done a job on the black man. However, there is a lot more to this than just the setback suffered because of imprisonment. Many permanent things should be pointed out here.

Four out of five black youths in some inner-city community can expect to be incarcerated in their lifetimes. Think about all the black men who have been detained and released since 1975. I am talking about those who are out of prison and coping with life now—like me, excluding the nearly one million locked up today.

How many black men have been stamped with an "X" on their back since 1975? Over 44 years, how many black men went through the system and are fortunate enough to still be alive on the streets? What is the number? Two, three, four, or five million black men maybe? I am not sure, but I bet it's high. I would be willing to go as far as to say more than 3,000,000 black men are walking the streets with X's on their backs. The Supreminati designed it this way.

You see, convicted felons are subject to accepted forms of discrimination reminiscent of the Jim Crow era. That includes being denied the right to vote, excluded automatically from serving on juries, and legally discriminated against in employment, housing, access to education, and certain public benefits. I can attest to this personally. I've been turned away from three jobs recently because of a criminal record stemming from 25-30 years ago.

In 2017, I was denied an apartment because of something that happened 30 years ago. Imagine how many black men are experiencing a similar situation. Remember, laws are designed strictly to put more blacks in prison—*daily*. Do you know the powder cocaine versus crack cocaine laws? These laws were designed to put black men in prison.

You see, if America really wanted a war against drugs, then anyone would know you battle that war at the borders. Why would they wait until it gets into all the households in the black communities? Because then the government has what they need to fill their slave camps with blacks they can arrest. The same practice goes with guns. Whites have many more guns than blacks do; whites also have a gun card registration. Blacks get them underground and go to jail for them.

The *three-strike* laws are for blacks. I am now seeing blacks getting written up for selling single cigarettes on the streets. How about those *stop and frisk* laws that enabled cops to stop people without any reasonable cause or suspicion? Who is that law for? To top it all off, they are trying to change the voting laws and take away our rights to vote. What is this country turning to?

Our government is a wicked regime; it's all about money and power. They *want drugs* in America. Also, it's not a coincidence that we are still in Afghanistan. 85% of the world's heroin comes from Afghanistan. What is the biggest drug problem in America today? Heroin use. The government began the pill epidemic maybe 10 years ago or so. All the doctors were prescribing Oxy-this and Oxy-that for anything and everything. They literally turned the citizens of the nation into junkies. What reason did we really need to stay over in Afghanistan other than the oil, plutonium, and heroin? On top of that, blacks get arrested for it and go to prison.

I hope black people will not sleep on the masterful and cleverly wicked schemes of The Supreminati. What is sad is this goes on every day in our lives. Many blacks have been put to sleep, and they are not aware of what this government has done to them—and is still doing to them.

Here They Are, Sisters

(Perhaps the Worst Crime of All – cont.)

How does the destruction of the black men affect sisters? Where does this leave them? Those who are saying there aren't enough qualified black men surely disqualify an ex-con as being qualified. You see, the experience of going to prison is an episode or an event, but life truly begins when one is released. Most brothers come out with a genuine intent to rebuild their lives, and in many cases, do the right thing, never wanting to see that hellhole again. However, now, the laws are stacked against him upon his release.

The rules are different for an ex-convict than they are for the average citizen. In most cases, it is hell trying to get back up on their feet. Most of the time, there is no support base waiting to assist the brothers. We walk on eggshells to avoid the petty confrontations from the (still-ignorant) blacks who haven't been in that system. More importantly, we continuously walk on eggshells to avoid going in front of a judge again. Participating in a bar fight can mean an extensive sentence for an ex-con. Not participating makes you a pussy in the eyes of your peers. It's a lose/lose proposition. The judge will let others go home with a slap on the wrist, but the guy with an "X" on his back (ex-con) will likely get sentenced to prison again. That is how the system works—another $30,000 in value to the state. Once he is labeled in that system, white judges will show no mercy. *Cha-Ching!*

The naked eyes of the sister cannot tune into how deliberate and real the forces against the brothers are when they are released. These forces are subtle, silent, and methodical. While many brothers are viewed as "nigga failures" to sisters, there are good brothers who come out of prisons. America keeps its foot in their ass in ways that are important to building the life that is necessary to building a healthy black family. It's a struggle to get a decent job because all the reliable companies do background checks. Trying to get an apartment is futile in most cases. Though I have never faced a criminal allegation involving a gun, I can't legally own a firearm to protect my family like the rest of American. Think about that for a minute. Everyone has the right to defend themselves under the Constitution except for people with a conviction. What does America want us to do now? We are talking about life and death.

The purpose is to prevent black men from being productive—period. People (overall) think it's chance, or lack of effort when our brothers come up short. I am not making excuses for the brothers; there are some lazy-asses in every crop. I get that, but if people cannot see this ploy is designed to ensure black men are targeted and destroyed in a way that will prevent them from becoming heads of households to complete black women's lives as an equal or greater yoked partner, then they are foolish and cannot see what is going on before them. That is a clever genocide. It is so smart that intelligent people cannot even recognize it!

That is the ultimate intent of curtailing the healthy reproduction of the entire black community:

- We have an original Constitution that once considered black people three-fifths human.
- We have a 13th Amendment to the Constitution that still permits slavery by the state after the conviction of a crime.
- We have (perhaps) 3,000,000 black men walking the streets tagged with "X's" on their backs.
- We have nearly 1,000,000 more still locked up.

- We have millions of well-accomplished and educated black women who have considerable voids in their lives, lacking an equal companion who aligns properly with their lifestyle.
- We have a broken community of black people.
- We have stymied people.

That is the ploy. It is how you break up and diminish a group of people. You destroy the union that produces healthy families. That is very strategic; this is cultural genocide, and you've got to admit the shit is clever. Until blacks approach this ill-treatment on a grand scale, collectively, with a strategy that resembles the magnitude and planning that went into constructing this horrible and cunning trick, then blacks may never correct it.

On the surface, one would think the black man is the direct target of the ploy. Actually, it is the black woman and family. He is merely the trigger. The black woman is the most damaging target. Through her, you can reach the entire community. How does the saying go? "The hand that rocks the cradle is the hand that rules the world."

Anyone who can think up such a ploy is also capable of thinking through its residual effect. It comes down to cause and effect. How would this affect the women, then how would she pass it on to the children, the grandchildren, and then ultimately, to her entire race? The black woman is the first teacher to the child. Therefore, if you want to influence the mass of people, you do it through the woman. If you have black women raising children to believe the girls are stronger than the boys, then you have literally altered the growth and development of an entire heritage of people. This practice is not in alignment with building a healthy family.

I truly don't think you can devise a plan of such magnitude without a vision of how those who love the black man would respond to it—the black woman. Then how those who love her would respond—the black children. Through this spiral effect, you are controlling the entire race. Again, the following is from the Willie Lynch letters:

THE BREAKING PROCESS OF THE AFRICAN WOMAN (emphasis added)

Take the female and run a series of tests on her to see if she will submit to your desires willingly. Test her in every way because she is the most important factor for good economics. If she shows any sign of resistance in submitting completely to your will, do not hesitate to use the bullwhip on her to extract that last bit of [b----] out of her. Take care not to kill her, for in doing so, you spoil good economics. When in complete submission, she will train her off springs in the early years to submit to labor when they become of age. Understanding is the best thing. Therefore, we shall go deeper into this area of the subject matter concerning what we have produced here in this breaking process of the female nigger. We have reversed the relationship; in her natural uncivilized state, she would have a strong dependency on the uncivilized nigger male, and she would have a limited protective tendency toward her independent male offspring and would raise male off springs to be dependent like her. Nature had provided for this type of balance. We reversed nature by burning and pulling a civilized nigger apart and bullwhipping the other to the point of death, all in her presence. By her being left alone, unprotected, with the MALE IMAGE DESTROYED, the ordeal caused her to move from her psychologically dependent state to a frozen, independent state. In this frozen, psychological state of independence, she will raise her MALE and female offspring in reversed roles. For FEAR of the young male's life, she will psychologically train him to be MENTALLY WEAK and DEPENDENT, but PHYSICALLY STRONG. Because she has become psychologically independent, she will train her

FEMALE offspring to be psychologically independent. What have you got? You've got the nigger WOMAN OUT FRONT AND THE nigger MAN BEHIND AND SCARED. This is a perfect situation of sound sleep and economics. Before the breaking process, we always had to be alertly on guard . Now, we can sleep soundly, for out of frozen fear, his woman stands guard for us. He cannot get past her early slave-molding process. He is a good tool, now ready to be tied to the horse at a tender age. By the time a nigger boy reaches the age of sixteen, he is soundly broken in and ready for a long life of sound and efficient work and the reproduction of a unit of good labor force. Continually, through the breaking of uncivilized savage niggers, by throwing the nigger female savage into a frozen psychological state of independence, by killing the protective male image, and by creating a submissive dependent mind of the nigger male slave, we have created an orbiting cycle that turns on its own axis forever, unless a phenomenon occurs and re-shifts the position of the male and female slaves. We show what we mean by example. Take the case of the two economic slave units and examine them close. (2009, FinalCall.com News)

The black woman holds the family together; she is the glue. She is naturally a divine vessel. For human life, God chose *her* to bring babies into this world. She has intelligence and breadwinning skills. She can do anything on earth because she is the bearer of life.

Consequently, the black man's importance in her life has been strategically reduced. The plan weakened the black man to the point where he is reduced in his purpose. Of course, not all black men because there are some success stories, but we are talking about the masses. Do not be pacified by the (fewer) success stories. Doing so will cause you to take your eyes off this tragedy, and you will start saying stupid shit like, "Black men are just lazy and don't want to do shit."

The black man's strength and ability to gain adequate employment to provide and be the leader of the black family do not come forth. This process caused the black man to come up short and perhaps, inferior psychologically in some regards. That is primarily due to his falling short of gaining proper guidance and maybe even higher education, and that is partially his own fault. Thus, he lost a great deal of respect from the black woman.

That is a very deviate and cunning thing to do to any group of people of any color. However, if your aim is to slow down and destroy their fruitful reproduction, then you start by dividing the man and woman. That creates conflict within the relationship between the two. Therefore, many blacks spend their time bumping heads like two rhinos. The black man is always fighting to regain the respect, power, and leadership bestowed upon him at birth. Still, then, the evil hands of The Supreminati stripped that away from him strategically.

As a result of her king being weakened, the black woman has been forced to fill in; some call it *hardened*. She was forced to carry the black family and maybe even the entire black race on her shoulders. *Thank God she did.* Because of this, her attitude is to take no shit from a black man. In fact, she seems to have less respect for him. She has low tolerance and patience for him as well. She may have slightly bought into the stereotypical reinforcement that America's media has placed on him: "The black man is lazy. He doesn't want to work. He always wants a handout." That is a viral victory for The Supreminati.

Neither the black woman nor the black man understands the evil ploy that has caused the division between the two. They may think it's just chance. I once saw a website that showed black men who were married to non-black women. (www.afieldnegro.com) The numbers are huge. The question here is, are black women chasing black men away. That did not happen by chance either; it happened by design. What a rotten thing for White Supreminati to do? Willie Lynch nailed it.

I am convinced many whites today have no clue how deep this is.

So, here we are, at war with each other like two alpha male-lions. War and love cannot occupy the same territory or space in the heart. Through love, we're able to be fruitful and multiply just as God would have it. Through war, we are divided, which is having a diminishing effect on us, just as the WLMF would have it.

The WLMF is still in effect today. Not only were blacks held back with over 400 years of slavery in this country, but also Willie Lynch created a virus he inserted into our subconscious hard-drives to sustain this evil plot for centuries. Then, America's white Supreminati carried on systematically with the genocide. They carried the baton.

This virus is designed to divide us in every possible way. Think about it. Aren't black people always saying, "Why can't blacks stick together like every other race of people?" I hear this so much from black people in America, but have you ever seen Ethiopians, Nigerians, Kenyans, or any other voluntary immigrant African groups here in the U.S. utilize this theory? No, they are so close as united people it amazes me. They are all knitted so well together I sometimes think they are all are blood-related.

I've concluded blacks *can* stick together; it is evident in the behavior of Africans who came voluntarily to this country. Remember Lynch said, "We have created an orbiting cycle that turns on its own axis forever unless a phenomenon occurs and re-shifts the position of the male and female slaves." That is powerful.

I truly don't believe whites are in tune or involved with the virus that keeps us working against our own people. This virus was inserted centuries ago. I do believe there remain white beliefs of white exceptionalism and privilege, and I'm also convinced some of them operate from a mindset that they are first-class and above the rest. Now think about it; this shit is embedded deeply within black people's subconscious and it has cunningly been woven in the conditioning and development of black people's psyche and behavior. I just don't think an average white mind today would care to investigate this deeply, nor would they care to evaluate the impact of the WLMF. I don't think most blacks even recognize why we are this way with each other. There must be an equally powerful strategy to counter what was done. If not, this virus will live forever.

Class War

(Final Thought on Politics)

I have heard people question whether Barack Obama's presidency caused more racism in this country. It is a very *off* question, but I understand where it is coming from. When you look at some of the behavior, outbursts, and disrespect shown towards President Obama from certain classes of whites in this country, it makes you wonder.

Remember, in 2009, when some white parents kept their children at home because Obama was visiting the schools? Remember when Congressman Joe Wilson burst out and called Obama a liar while he was speaking to a Joint Session of Congress? Remember, during the McCain campaign, when the old white lady stood up and accused Obama of being a terrorist? John McCain stood up and said to the lady, "No, he is a good family man. We disagree on a lot of policies, but he is a good, respectable man."

Let me mention that what John McCain did was good. He stopped the hate the woman was trying to stir up. Had it been Trump, I bet he would have egged it on and stirred it up among a group that would have cheered and promoted hate. That's the difference between preaching politics and preaching hate.

What about *former* Arizona Governor, Jan Brewer pointing her finger in President Obama's face and countless other acts that occurred daily, especially seen on Fox News? I shouldn't call it news, but rather, the alt-right channel.

What about Donald Trump and President Obama's birth certificate pursuit? What is most scary to me is that Trump is not a politician. To me, he is a businessman turned entertainer. His business sense, combined with his understanding of T.V. ratings (and how to play them), is what helped him into office. *Politics became dirtier than ever this time.*

The dumbing down of America was officially achieved by putting Donald Trump in office. What's really sad is that our country would even elect him as the president. Again, he is brilliant, but his brilliance is used for mischief. He understands America's appetite for sleazy T.V. and turned the election into a Jerry Springer show—combined with the fact that our Republicans are so fed up with their own leaders.

The acts from white people against President Obama were very extreme, wouldn't you say? Have you ever seen reactions of such hateful natures directed toward any other president in the history of this country? The president visiting a school has been like a royal occasion for any school in the history of this nation. Screaming out, "You're a liar!" to a president is unheard of. Shouldn't he have gotten escorted out for disrespecting the office or the institution of the presidency?

Pointing a finger in President Obama's face is equally unfathomable. Shouldn't Michelle Obama have the right to step outside her classy and respectful demeanor for a moment and, excuse me, have "gotten off into Jan Brewer's ass" for the total disrespect shown towards her husband? These acts from white people (to me) were like saying, "Yeah, you're the president, but you still need to answer to us, nigger." What really is this? Were they saying, "You are still just a nigger," or "We are still the first-class people ahead of you, no matter what your title is?"

Honestly, I believe they were saying both. Whites were indirectly saying in their mind: *who in the hell do you think you are? You are still just a nigger president.* The office of the presidency lost a great deal of its majestic and honorable stature because of this disrespect to President Obama. I saw something worthy of noting here. For once, the majesty of that position was lowered. Black people saw this as ascending to a higher plateau and being something worthy of admiration, a breaking of the racial *glass ceiling*. However, the Alt-Right re-adjusted the ceiling. They downgraded a great deal of its majesty and esteem. In an extreme sense, it was almost as if "now that you, Black Man, are in it that position (presidency), it ain't really shit no more." As if to say, "Fuck that institution of the presidency of the United States; we still run this shit anyway."

In essence, white America lowered the bar or the ceiling. All the disrespectful, ugly, and nasty treatment of President Obama consequently re-adjusted the prestige, dignity, and integrity of the position. As if to say, "Let us show you what's really going on, or who really fits here." To me, this says the allegiance is not to a capable, qualified figure (to diligently carry out the responsibilities that accompany the position), the loyalty is to our clique, and that clique is White Supremacy—to put it in a Jay-Z lyrical format. Remind us to re-introduce ourselves; the name is White Supremacy.

I imagine it took a black man as the face of this country to bring out the truth and remove the gray areas of our society. President Obama caused everyone to run to their corners. Like what Bernie Mac says at the beginning of *The Bernie Mac show*, "Who you with?"

Everyone was forced to represent what group they truly belong to. That is not just a black and white issue; it is a *class issue*. We are what we are—period! Even poor whites have a better understanding of where they stand in the country now. Also, middle-class whites have been slotted more definitively into their place. All the lines are cut and dry now:

- Women understand the stance on equal pay to men.
- All the battle lines have been drawn regarding abortion, same-sex unions, transvestites, and immigration.

I have never seen the interest of the various groups *of citizens* as crystallized and pronounced as they are today. The recession seems to have created the prelude to a class revolution. Everyone's true position and platform had to come to the forefront. It took a black man like President Obama to bring it all out, so the question of whether President Obama's presidency caused more racism is not exactly the right one to ask. Consider that just maybe a black face is what it took to force the truth out of everyone, whites especially. Therefore, his presidency didn't create more racism; it just crystallized it!

I've also heard a few blacks say things like, "He is in bed with the Wall Street people." It is also stated he hasn't done enough for black people. I do have my thoughts on this as well.

Many know Wall Street is tied to the Federal Reserve families. Goldman Sachs allegedly collects interest on American debt. The Federal Reserve families run the entire country, in my opinion. That is the nucleus of The Supreminati.

I am amazed at how these people stay under the radar without blame for the **tragic** conditions and events that have happened in this country and around the world. People should wrap their minds around the fact that they *literally* make all money. That is not a metaphor nor an exaggeration; this is a literal fact. They have absolute control over almost every aspect of American life. That is the real power.

I once read a book called *Confessions of an Economic Hit Man* by John Perkins. If you want to know how corrupt the U.S. power structure is, you can get a scary insight from a guy who resigned from the government because his conscience could no longer take working for them anymore.

The Wall Streeters are an extension of the interest of the Federal Reserve families. Goldman Sachs, J.P Morgan-Chase, and Bank of America are on the front line. For black people who attack President Obama in the media, do they really think he was the boss of the U.S.A.? Are they familiar with the Trilateral Commission? The Lehman's, the Warburg's, the Rothschilds, the Rockefellers, the Counsel Foreign on Relations, the Bohemian Group, Skull and Bones, Kuhn Loeb, and all the others that make up the Federal Reserve and The Supreminati? This 8,000-pound gorilla influences every aspect of American life, from the military and mass weaponry decisions to the drug trade, the oil trade, precious metals, the media, pharmaceutical industry, hi-tech, all stock exchanges, and agriculture.

To me, it is stupid to say Barrack was in bed with Wall Street. Maybe it's more fitting to say the institution of the presidency is in bed with Wall Street. Remember, our country banks with the Federal Reserve. They only wanted his face on the front of America, behind Bush. It seems like no matter who the president is, there are 10 or more people from Goldman Sachs who are fixtures in the President's cabinet. The Federal Reserve was established in 1913—the same year the IRS was formed. *Hmmm. It makes one think!*

It is more fitting to say the Federal Reserve families make the bed for the entire nation because they print the money. In other words, the entire country is their bed. They allow us to play in it with the *illusion of inclusion,* as brother Umar Johnson would say. President Obama was no exception.

My overall take is that I love and totally respect our brother, President Obama. He seems to have the brilliance that stands alone. His intelligence is enormous. I believe God was with him, and that's good enough for me. Many of his black critics in the media should not have assassinated his character. He didn't run on a Dr. Martin Luther King platform. Dr. King died 50-something years ago, and America has changed drastically since his death. Therefore, blacks should not have expected President Obama to turn into Dr. King.

The truth is, I don't think Dr. Martin Luther King Jr. could have ever become president in the U.S. America doesn't care about a black man's agenda. I am not limiting Dr. King's vision. It was about justice for all people. That is not the agenda of The Supreminati; controlling present-day America is.

Given the circumstances, President Obama did a phenomenal job. He came into a basketball game down 50 points at half time, dealing with an America that no other president in the history of this country had ever seen. I am not just talking about the economy. It is the polarization and racial hatred, along with many other things exclusive to his presidency.

I will admit his eight-year tenure was a feel-good moment for black people. However, it's unfortunate that the agenda of The Supreminati was best served with a black face on the front of America. To a large degree, President Obama was played by them, and he gets a bad rap from many blacks for not doing enough. He also gets a bad rap for foreign activities that took place under his watch. I am smart enough to know he wasn't the real power. He was the fall guy. At the end of the day, he is still viewed as a good man, and that is why people seem to still love the guy.

Some of our intelligent blacks in politics should get real about what is going on here. We've heard the term "United States of America Incorporated." The Presidency is a position within. The term is four, maybe eight years. Some corporations have a board and a C.E.O. They usually have more power than the President. *I'm just saying.*

Do you remember the time when Hilary Clinton and President Obama was detoured from a scheduled event to attend a secret meeting with some secret people? Hilary even came back and said, "We were told what we are gonna do," referring to the fact that she and Barack were just given some instructions. My point is this: let's not be stupid. There are powers that surrounds those the public thinks have the power. These are the real Powers to me. "The Supreminati" is what I call them.

Re-Shifting the Axis

Despite the damages done by these horrible acts emanating from WLMF, I find something particularly good coming out from it: God allows us to occupy His world. The horrors blacks have endured have pushed and forced many to be closer to God with less reliance on man. I believe the ultimate reward or accomplishment in life is closeness to God; it is the height of one's existence. A strong relationship with God is paramount to all things on this planet called Earth.

What if:

Barrack and Michelle Obama, David Icke, Ken

O'Keeffe (not the popular coach; the ex-Marine who renounced his citizenship), Oprah Winfrey, Bob Johnson, Lebron James, Michael Jordan, TD Jakes, Dr. Claude Anderson, Noel Jones, Pastor Byron Brazier from Chicago, Sheila Johnson, Berry Gordy, Quincy Jones, Beyoncé, Debra Lee, Colin Powell, Janice Bryant Holroyd, the Rev. Al Sharpton, Russell Simmons, the Rev. Jessie Jackson, Harry Belafonte, Dr, Boyce Watkins, Tavis Smiley, Umar Johnson, Cornell West, Stevie Wonder, Morgan Freeman, Spike Lee, Michael Eric Dyson, John Singleton, Eddie Murphy, Will Smith, Tyler Perry, Denzel Washington, Magic Johnson, Shaquille O'Neal, Jay Z, Diddy, Dr. Dré, LL Cool J, Master P, KRS-One, Chuck D, Snoop Dog, Ice T, Tom Joyner, Ice Cube, Common, Samuel L. Jackson, 50 Cent, Kanye West, Queen Latifah, Halle Berry, Maxine Waters, Wendy Williams, Chris Rock, Steve Harvey, Lupe Fiasco. Kendrick Lamar, Kevin Garnett, Kirk Franklin, Donnie McClurkin, Justice Clarence Thomas, Yolanda

Adams, Michael Baisden, Monique, Warren Ballentine, AC Green (radio host), Rev Run, Louis Farrakhan, and many others decided to collaborate and become the phenomenon to reset Black Life here in America? I tell you; a nucleus of this magnitude could be the phenomenon. Many other black men and women could be included here.

The effort put forth must match or even surpass the impact that Willie Lynch's teachings had on those slave owners because those slave owners went back to their camps and instilled these teachings into millions of black people. Therefore, make no mistake about it; blacks need most blacks on deck.

Many times, blacks have made isolated efforts to address specific issues in the communities. Separate matters are good, but they do not have the impact necessary to affect this. As Willie Lynch stated, *it will take a phenomenon to re-shift the axis.*

The same man who taught whites the art of nailing

blacks to a life-long state of self-destruction also gave us the way out of it. A phenomenon is what it will take. *Let's do the Phenomenon!* If such a group of black people decided to come together on this, it could be like the rebirth of a Black Wall Street, but 25 times broader. Do you remember Black Wall Street? Did you know the only bomb ever dropped on an American city from an airplane was by white supremacist who dropped it on a thriving black district in the early 1900s? They literally bombed blacks from the air.

The date was June 1, 1921, when "Black Wall Street," the name was fittingly given to one of the most affluent all-black communities in America, was bombed from the air and burned to the ground by mobs of white racist officials, Klansmen, and other envious white groups. In a period spanning fewer than 12 hours, a once-thriving 36-block black business district in northern Tulsa, Oklahoma laid smoldering. A model community was destroyed, and a major African-American economic movement resoundingly defused.

'Black (Negro) Wall Street' was the name given, by Booker T. Washington, to Greenwood Avenue of North Tulsa, Oklahoma, during the early 1900s. Because of strict segregation, "Negroes" were only allowed to shop, spend, and live in a 35-square block area called the Greenwood district. The *circulation of Black dollars only* in the black community produced a tremendously prosperous black business district. It was admired and envied by the whole country for its 21 churches, 21 restaurants, 30 grocery stores, and two movie theaters, plus a hospital, a bank, a post office, libraries, schools, law offices, a half-dozen private airplanes, and even a bus system. It was a time when the entire state of Oklahoma had only two airports, yet six blacks owned their own planes. It was a fascinating community. The area encompassed over 600 businesses and 36 square blocks with a population of 15,000 African Americans. They burned it down. They hated black people. White supremacy still hates black people today; they just mask it better.

The best description of Black Wall Street, or Little Africa as it was also known, would be to liken it to a mini-Beverly Hills. As far as resources, there were men and women with Doctorate of Philosophy degrees (Ph.D.'s) residing in Little Africa, along with black attorneys and black doctors.

One doctor, Dr. Berry, also owned the bus system. His average income was $500 a day, a hefty sum in 1910. During that era, physicians owned medical schools. It was the golden door of the black community during the early 1900s, and it proved that African Americans had a successful infrastructure. The dollar circulated 36 to 1,000 times, sometimes taking a year for currency to leave the community. Conversely, in 2019, a dollar leaves the black community in 15 minutes.

https://officialblackwallstreet.com/black-wall-street-story/

I would really like to see the rebirth of Black Wall Street. Today, the Phenomenon would be unstoppable. This time around, it would live on. It would be a beautiful time for the progress of black people and black families.

The fact is, the black man must rebuild himself, his family, his goals, and his desires. He has been systematically destroyed in this country. Since he was the trigger and first target of The Supreminati, he must be the first target to be reestablished in a rebirth. This rebuilding must be on a massive scale for it to sustain momentum. Little small isolated efforts will not cut it. It will take a Phenomenon with dedication. Many dis-enfranchised black men with X's on their backs must return to a better life.

The Supreminati will not forgive them. They will keep blacks disqualified for many things with criminal background checks that will last the rest of their lives. Blacks must free their own kind from America's plague on black men. We must train them for stable careers that only black people would care to see them with.

How much would it cost to start 25 black districts in 25 urban areas for blacks today? I don't know, but I honestly believe if a nucleus of the group mentioned wanted to do it, it could change the path the entire black community has been on for decades. Let's start with 25 black districts in 25 of our most depressed areas: Chicago, Detroit, Los Angeles, Cleveland, Baltimore, Atlanta, DC, Jackson, Memphis, Miami Gardens, New Orleans, Montgomery, Savannah, Philadelphia, New York, Dallas, Albany, Flint, Macon, etc.

Maybe I'm just a dreamer. It is sad to think the WLMF divides us all, even at the highest levels of fame and fortune. We could learn something from the Jews after the Holocaust. They decided to work together and ensure their kind would always support each other. They were not reprogrammed in the manner blacks were. Blacks were brainwashed. The Jews' tragedy was different, but afterward, they decided collectively to support each other and ensure they would thrive economically, and they did. Look at them now; they control their own destiny.

Remember, in the words of Willie Lynch, "If executed properly, it will last for hundreds, maybe even thousands of years." Our tragedy was designed to be long-term and has kept blacks in a self-destructive and divisive mode successfully. Again, I repeat myself, "He nailed it."

Blacks could start with establishing a $5 billion kitty to finance the 25 black districts. If 1,000 millionaires donated $5MM to the movement, this would be a financial beginning for rebuilding. Or if 5,000 millionaires donated $1 million each, blacks would have seed money via *private funds*. To hell with the U.S. government! It is time to set out to design 25 black districts in 25 of our major depressed cities.

Each district would consist of black-owned schools, hospitals, attorneys, insurance companies, and banks, with barbershops, salons, grocery stores, churches, restaurants, retail, and wholesale stores. Transportation could also be included, anywhere from black Uber-like drivers to black-owned busses. That would be a starting point.

The black dollar must be concentrated to support black businesses. That is how people can rebuild their community—employ black men! I am not sure of the cost to do any of this, but within the nucleus, there are the skillsets to address every area of expertise necessary to figure out the strategy. Claude Anderson, Dr Boyce Watkins and Minister Farrahkan should lead this project. What could stop it?

Even whites could donate to the kitty. Many white

organizations donate to the United Negro College Fund (UNCF), as well as other black programs; I'm sure some of them would be willing to participate. Any white, brown, yellow, or red organization could donate to the kitty. Good white people have remorse for what their ancestors have done to the downtrodden and oppressed black people. The cotton trade and slavery are the reasons for the wealth of many white families today.

Reparations will probably never happen for black people. We can't open casinos. I believe this is the only way to begin leveraging the power of the black dollar. Instead of only continuing to seek fairness from The Supreminati, what about using the Jewish playbook?

Can many black powerhouse people collaborate to achieve this Phenomenon? Can this be done with all the varied interests of blacks with wealth in this country? Would their differences be too divisive to enable this to happen? Is tending to their daily business too important than sacrificing the time, money, and energy to accomplish this monumental thing that could potentially change the world? Can this become their daily business? I repeat:

To all the powerful and influential blacks in business, politics, sports, academia, music, and the arts,

Will you make this your daily business, your legacy to America, and our youths?

If blacks are not willing to match the effort that all the slave owners put in to implement the evil teachings from Willie Lynch, then should my people honestly expect to turn things around? What those slave owners did was phenomenal. It was wicked but phenomenal. They learned a trade, and then they instilled what they learned into an entire mass of people. Can blacks ever match that effort to counter all the damage that was done?

In terms of physics, it's time the *immovable object*

(of institutional racism) encounters the *irresistible force* (of the black Phenomenon). Is the greatest damage from the virus also found in those at the top of the black success chain—in those who collectively have the power to change things?

To me, at the bottom of the black food chain, our differences turn into gang wars, hate, and violence, which produce the state in which we see in our ghettos today. On the other hand, at the top of our black food chain, our differences seem to create a different kind of disaster. It is an inability to collaborate. Maybe it is **ego**. Someone once told me E.G.O. was an acronym for Edging God Out. Is the ego too big to humble down? That is as bad a tragedy as the state of young blacks killing each other in our streets. The inability of powerful blacks to collaborate for this cause to fix it, maybe even worse of a tragedy. I say this because this group collectively working may be the only force powerful enough on Earth today to provide the

Phenomenon necessary to re-shift the axis Willie Lynch spoke about.

If, in the 20th century, whites collaborated successfully to destroy the black group, can blacks collaborate in the 21st century successfully to fix it? Are blacks too busy with their daily lives? Is the virus still working on every level of the black success chain? Can blacks meet up at a river to begin undoing this mess, tragedy, and horrible actions?

What would it mean to all the hopeless fatherless young black teens who have resorted to gangs, drugs, and violence to see such powerful and admired blacks coming back to re-shift this axis that white supremacists set as a trap? Most would be extremely edified to see this if they are sensible.

I look at it like this: we can form a few corporations around one mission. That is a business venture with the expectation of real profits. The profits are almost a certainty when you think about the black dollar. Right now, the black dollar is running wild, supporting every other nationality. This move would concentrate those dollars into the black community. It would enrich the black business community tremendously.

I heard once the spending power of the black community is north of $1 trillion. The wealth that will come from keeping the black dollar circulating within the black business community will not only benefit the lower-class blacks. It can be structured in a way that makes all the black donating participants earn more profit, thereby increasing their wealth. Those blacks who have money can act in the role of a seed or angel investor, or a supposed "Private Reserve" of this new black economy. If a black person is worth $10 million, then this investment could return them a profit of five or tenfold after 10 years. It would be the best stock in the market.

Blacks could structure this "Private Reserve" under the proper investment vehicle so it makes sense. Perhaps a REIT, a Real Estate Investment Trust, or a joint venture. This vehicle and transaction can divide earnings proportionately according to the donation amount. In this way, their gains or dividends are tied proportionately to the growth and success of the project. I am not an expert on this investment vehicle, but I believe it can be done. The necessary expertise is found within the nucleus.

It's a shame many great black businesses have been sold to whites, such as BET (Black Entertainment Television), and that Johnson Products and Motown are no longer black-owned. These phenomenal accomplishments, created and started by black people, have been sold off to whites because white people saw that they were powerful ventures. Blacks now purchase black hair care products. We now buy hair/weaves from the Koreans at their shops. The Vietnamese have a nail shop on every black corner nationwide. It is sad that almost every nationality of people has sold or is selling something to blacks. What are black people selling? Not much. I hear blacks complain about foreigners coming into the neighborhoods, opening grocery stores, gas stations, clothing, and liquor stores. Are blacks just professional customers to any group that wants to get rich?

Believe me, the Indians from Calcutta are getting rich from our people. In India, poverty prevails abundantly, but Indians come to America, open gas stations, motels, convenience stores, and become wealthy from the black U.S. residents. Will blacks ever stop waiting on a white supremacist nation to show some remorse and fix their own problems?

The good thing is that collectively, blacks have the power to affect the change necessary to transform their path. I really hope the damages from the Willie Lynch teachings are not preventing our wealthiest, most powerful, and influential blacks from working together. I also hope the suggestion of starting 25 black districts is found to be great and a starting point to our most powerful and influential blacks.

I am asking whites and other nationalities if they would support this idea, especially if they are not opposed to reparations. Go to the website www.thesupreminati.com and share your opinions on reparations for black people and how you feel about blacks building districts to re-create and support an economic infrastructure.

White supremacy is black people's eighth most deadly sin. It is the father of racism. Dr. King spoke about the "Promised Land." I think blacks should start building it. It will be like a 10-ton bowling ball that is difficult to push. However, if all prominent, successful, wealthy, and influential blacks got behind the bowling ball and puuuuussshhhhed together, the burden that blacks are plagued with would begin to roll off. It is 10 times easier to keep the ball rolling than it is to get it going, but it will take a helluva push to get it started. Once it starts, the momentum would quickly move blacks into a more productive and beautiful state of living.

This one act would literally change the course and destiny for an entire group of people. It would be *phenomenal!* Pushing together and building together would solve the puzzle so our people can then revise the old song sang during the civil rights era to we **have** overcome. It will take a Phenomenon, just as Willie Lynch said.

When you think about the struggles of the many successful blacks in this country, each story is unique. All these people are phenomenal in their own way. If you joined all these extraordinary people together in a concerted effort to rewrite and execute the correct blueprint for the black community, it would restart life in this land of America. It could be the *Restart button* that blacks need to re-shift the axis.

I suppose God would give a sigh of relief that blacks finally used the power He gave us. My spirit tells me He would bless the act with an enormous amount of grace and favor... then maybe show blacks a smile through the heavenly sky.

The order is tall, and I once considered it far too remote. I presume now blacks have become so fed up in this country, the pursuit of such a Phenomenon could be seriously entertained. Reparation checks might be off the table. Blacks need to be the Phenomenon to re-shift the axis.

Let's face it; blacks have been asking for help for a long time in this country. We should accept *it is what it is*, we are told. Instead of putting too much energy into seeking change from The Supreminati, we must fix the problem they inflicted upon us, and let God do the rest. That is 2020. We've had occurrences like the Travon Martin, Michael Brown, Erik Gardner, and now George Floyd incidents. We have new stop and frisk laws targeting black men in some states. I could go on with many things designed to negatively impact blacks in urban areas. What can we really do? Keep asking for fairness? We will, but isn't it obvious what they think of black life? While we can march, picket, and demonstrate under our rights as U.S. citizens, it will only get us another compromise from The Supreminati (if we are lucky).

Having a war between blacks and whites in America would not be smart because the country is in a very fragile state financially. White supremacists are stockpiling guns and ammo, preparing for some kind of Armageddon while many blacks are struggling with and consumed by the daily trials of poverty. The biggest reality here is that all the laws are now in place for the U.S. government to declare martial law. Therefore, if a revolution should ever happen, blacks would be out-gunned.

The Bush administration established new laws, including the Patriot Act and the Insurrection Act, which allows for the U.S. president to deploy troops within the U.S. to put down insurrection, lawlessness, and rebellion. While Dr. Martin Luther King was Christ-like in his way of trying to work things out peacefully so that we could live together in parity and equality, I don't think white supremacists can share such a lifestyle unless they heal.

While Malcolm X seemed to approach things with an acceptance that whites would never love thy brother and that blacks should maybe seek alternative means for equality, I, too, believe white supremacists are not interested in loving thy brother. However, many white people want to heal and just don't know how to go about it.

What options do blacks have if we genuinely want to fix the black race? Isn't it time we stop kidding ourselves and take things seriously? To offset or shock the Willie Lynch effect and throw it off its axis, we must do something as phenomenal as what he did.

I realize I am a dreamer, but my dreams extend even further. I've learned that for alcoholics or drug addicts to begin the process of healing, we must first admit and *accept that we have a problem*. While ordinary white people know racism is real, they seem to think when slavery ended, we could just *turn the page*. That is where the problem becomes dangerous. They tend to believe the page was turned from that chapter, and it was only a serious problem *yesterday*. That is why racism is so bad today. It's never treated like the illness it truly is.

Racist is like a drug addict, not understanding he is a dope fiend. Therefore, he does nothing about it. The same thing goes for white people. The side effects of racism are not painful to most of them. You would think the evidence of damaged and unhappy black people would be enough of a side effect to make whites spend more time looking inward at their disease, with the intended purpose of healing or fixing their problem. Obviously not.

Is it possible we will ever see treatment or a prescription for the disease of racism? Is it enough of a problem for whites to ever have them apply any effort (whatsoever) to first understand the degree and ugliness of their wickedness and its impact on black people? Or, am I just dreaming again? I'm asking whites in general, and all nationalities to give their opinion on a program like Racism Anonymous. Again, if you haven't already, then go to www.thesupreminati.com. Click on the Forum section and give your opinion about a program like this. Your opinions are valuable.

I believe The Supreminati is truly the power that runs the United States of America and the world. Further, if we look into federal reserve families, Bohemian Grove attendees, the Council on Foreign Relations, the Zionist, free-masonry, Rothschild, Skull and Bones, The Bilderberg Group, and several other secret organizations of wealth, we will find many commonalities amongst them. New World Order would be one for sure, and I'd bet my life the systematic and cunning destruction of black people is always on their daily To-Do list.

I cannot see white supremacists ever giving a shit to fix the damages brought upon the black community. At some point, blacks must put forth much less effort on pleading for absolute fairness and re-direct that energy to self-repair. Just as the black woman once said, "To hell with the black man. I don't need no man to do shit for me," the black race collectively needs to take this attitude towards the U.S Government. I assume our people would then uplift and soar, just as the black woman did. We must love our country while hating what it did to us at the same time.

White people, in general, are needed to join blacks in trying to rid the hate from these Oligarchs. Let's get rid of The Supreminati by taking away their power and influence. These people are so rich they live in a different world far from us. Yet they cause us to war with each other to execute whatever evil schemes they have for the world entirely. Non-racist whites are the closest to these Oligarchs. They should stand with blacks to aggressively fight all the racism and hate that comes from the supremacists and The Supreminati. They must publicly stand against it. Such a stand will have a swift impact on eradicating this disease, destroying our world.

To some degree, I see white Americans are starting to publicly stand against them. Thanks to Donald Trump, ordinary whites can no longer ignore the presence and impact of The Supreminati and the hate that comes from white supremacy. Non-racist whites are starting to feel the hate. The Supreminati is doing a number on them as well. Welcome to our world. At the end of the day, it boils down to classism. Either you are in with them, or you are not.

I stated earlier that Trump is a blessing to black people. The Supreminati historically has operated with truly little attention on them. The hate and damage they inflicted on this world went on somewhat unnoticed in the public eye. I suppose the white supremacists were so angered that a black man won the presidency of this country, they showed us their displeasure by putting one of theirs into office. At their rallies, they were clowning. Those celebrations were beyond a political win. They were like a party was going on, and they *were free to come out of the white supremacist closet.* They felt so embolden that an old white man snuck up on a young black protester and hit him in the face. Afterward, the cops, or fellow supremacist members, roughed up and arrested the young black guy.

Can you believe Donald Trump once said he never heard of David Duke? I can say blacks are gaining an ally, and that ally is the non-racist white folks. Unfortunately, they needed to feel some pain and hate. Donald Trump brought it to them by totally isolating and crystallizing white power.

You might think I'm kidding, but I can identify (in my relationship with a few ordinary white folks) improvements for the better. It's like the hoods have been pulled off the faces of supremacists, and The Supreminati is now exposed. Ordinary white people realized they don't like them either. That enables me to imagine a world without the hate that comes from both. That is the beginning of dealing with hate.

Moreover, let me digress for a moment. The Hip Hop genre, created by blacks, might just have the greatest impact on driving out racism. Think about this; by the time Eminem is 80 years of age, his peers and those around his age would have grown up in the Hip Hop era. All the elite positions in politics, banking, criminal justice, every field, or profession will be occupied by white people who grew up during the Hip Hop era, even the police force.

These young whites will not treat blacks as second-class people. I cannot see them interacting in the meanspirited way their ancestors did. They grew up rockin' to Public Enemy, NWA, Common, and the Ghetto Boyz. Many of the white girls of generation X, Y, and Z are turned on by rappers. I am surprised at how cool some of the young white boys have become since being introduced to the Hip Hop culture. They've got *swag*. They quote Rap lyrics word for word. I've even heard some of them refer to each other with the expression "my nigga." The influence of hate and racism should dissipate of old age. Like everything else, there will still be some racist individuals, but mostly, they will all die off.

To all the young blacks from New York who created Rap and Hip Hop, not only did you create a great genre of music, but also your creation will have a divine impact in the world. You may have created the culture that will weaken or perhaps replace this racist society. Hip Hop has brought many young people together. As the older white supremacists die, the emergence of the new generation will come in. Hip Hop is one arena where all nationalities of people can attend the party that black people hosted.

Hip Hop will become a senior citizen someday. They say Father Time is undefeated. Versus hate and racism, I'm putting my money on Father Time. I just hope he steps out of character and hurry.

God is love. Despite the religious and political differences we have in this world, if we tried love (God's kind), love would fix all things. It would first remove the hate that fuels racism. Then, as a human race (black and white people) strapped with the love of God, we can destroy The Supreminati (aka Satan's Committee).

We have failed to have peace and equality.

I have a message to The Supreminati, America, and the powerful people who influence the lives of its citizens. You cannot keep or hold a people down without staying down there with them. You cannot soar like the eagle you reference so often as the representation of this country. Karma is like the universe's built-in tracking device. The eagle is trying to soar with its sins of racism and slavery tied to its wings like bricks. How can we claim to be a Christian nation if we refuse to exercise a fundamental tenant of Christianity to simply ask forgiveness from those you have wronged?

I believe God knew we would forget how to love each other unconditionally. Maybe He spelled his name backward and put it on four legs to remind us each day when we return home what love feels like. Jesus said, "Love thy neighbor." Can we truly try this—from one person to the other person, country to country, continent to continent? It is the one thing we seem to have forgotten how to do. We've had so little practice in exercising this act of our will that we truly don't know how to anymore. In it all, where is Racism Anonymous?

…Reshifting the axis of hate. I have a dream, too.

THE END (FOR NOW)

References

CBS News, Jack and Jill Politics, and The Root, Passed Health Care Reform (Affordable Care Act)

As reported by the blog "Jack and Jill Politics," Blacks will enjoy several benefits that the bill provides:

More than 19 percent of African Americans do not have health care, according to The Root. When the highly debated health care reform bill was signed into law in March of 2010, millions of African Americans benefited.

The Grio, Expanded Funding for HBCUs

In February of this year, President Obama signed an executive order increasing funding for Historically Black Colleges and Universities (HBCUs) to $850 million over the next 10 years. The funding is being administered through the White House Initiative on Historically Black Colleges and Universities that was, ironically, started by the late Ronald Reagan.

The Huffington Post, Awarded $1.2 Billion to Black

Farmers

> President Obama's administration oversaw the $1.2
> billion settlement awarded to Black farmers who
> have been denied loans and assistance by the
> Agricultural Dept. for decades.

The New York Times, CBS News, Created the Civil Rights
Division of the Justice Department

> The U.S. Justice Department is leading one of the
> most aggressive defenses of civil rights in recent
> memory. Whether it is clamping down on Arizona
> for its bias against Latinos or fighting unjust state
> voter ID laws, this Justice Department has been
> fully engaged in fighting for the rights of all
> minorities. When President Obama chose Eric
> Holder to lead the department, he picked a true
> champion of civil rights. For a rundown of how
> powerful the Civil Rights Division has become,
> check out this article by The Root.

Tyson, Timothy, The Blood of Emmet Till

The Washington Post, Signed the Crack Cocaine Bill (Fair
Sentencing Act)

Crack users are disproportionately sentenced to longer jail terms than those who use powder. This unfair sentencing practice punished African Americans more severely than their white counterparts. With the signing of the Fair Sentencing Act, though, President Obama narrowed that disparity significantly.

"Signed the Democratic-sponsored Credit Card Accountability, Responsibility and Disclosure (CARD) Act, which was designed to protect consumers from unfair and deceptive credit card practices." http://1.usa.gov/gIaNcS

"Initiated a $15 billion plan designed to encourage increased lending to small businesses." http://1.usa.gov/eu0u0b

"Through the American Recovery and Reinvestment Act, saved at least 300,000 education jobs, such as teachers, principals, librarians, and counselors that would have otherwise been lost." http://1.usa.gov/ez30D

"Ordered all federal contractors to pay a minimum wage of $10.10 per hour, leading the way to a national increase." http://wapo.st/1iaU5kd

"Brought the housing market all the way back from total collapse, to create a rally for housing starts."
http://reut.rs/1NTAOVUhttp://reut.rs/1NTAOVU

"By signing Dodd-Frank legislation, created the Consumer Financial Protection Bureau" http://1.usa.gov/j5onG

"Signed the American Jobs and Closing Tax Loopholes Act, which closed many of the loopholes that allowed companies to send jobs overseas and avoid paying US taxes by moving money offshore." http://1.usa.gov/qbd1RTq

https://www.biography.com/people/john-brown-9228496

https://timeline.com/jackie-robinson-wouldnt-go-to-the-back-of-the-bus-bd637b346c3f

https://aaregistry.org/story/william-still-philadelphia-abolitionist

http://www.usa-exile.org/news/0306/02/elitefedfamilies.html

http://news.bbc.co.uk/2/shared/spl/hi/uk/06/prisons/html/nn2page1.stm)

http://www.rense.com, 2009

http://www.ecclesia.org/Lawgiver/PDF/nbn2P.pdf

http://www.bibleprobe.com/abortion.htm

http://www.blackgenocide.org/black.html

www.statista.com/statistics/666862/african-american-buying-power-in-the-us/

About the Author

Born in Chicago, Illinois, **Coleman G. Lauderdale** was raised in the south suburban area of East Chicago Heights, also known as Ford Height. Having served a little over eight years in prison, he was jailed on two separate occasions for two different crimes. These experiences have given him an in-depth and broad perspective on the inner workings of social engineering that shaped and conditioned his life. While Coleman's story is semi-autobiographical, the correlation with many of his experiences is mirrored with many other black lives that matter.